FORCE and MOTION

PHYSICS IN OUR WORLD

FORCE and MOTION

Kyle Kirkland, Ph.D.

Facts On File
An imprint of Infobase Publishing

FORCE AND MOTION

Facts On File, Inc.
An imprint of Infobase Publishing
132 West 31st Street
New York NY 10001

ISBN-10: 0-8160-6111-4 **07-08**
ISBN-13: 978-0-8160-6111-2

Library of Congress Cataloging-in-Publication Data

07-08 FF 33.98

Kirkland, Kyle.
   Force and motion / Kyle Kirkland.
156   p. cm.—(Physics in our world)
   Includes bibliographical references and index.
   ISBN 0-8160-6111-4 (acid-free paper)
   1. Force and energy. 2. Motion. I. Title. II. Series.
   QC73.K57 2007
   531'.6—dc22   2006012551

Facts On File books are available at special discounts when purchased in bulk quantities for businesses, associations, institutions, or sales promotions. Please call our Special Sales Department in New York at (212) 967-8800 or (800) 322-8755.

You can find Facts On File on the World Wide Web at http://www.factsonfile.com

Text design by Kerry Casey
Cover design by Dorothy M. Preston
Illustrations by Dale Williams

Printed in the United States of America

MP FOF 10 9 8 7 6 5 4 3 2 1

This book is printed on acid-free paper.

This book is dedicated to Dr. Jesse L. Kirkland (1931–2006), who applied his knowledge of physics and engineering mechanics while working for NASA and the Department of Defense. To my regret, he was a man and father I never really knew.

❉ CONTENTS ❉

✺ PREFACE ✺

THE NUCLEAR BOMBS that ended World War II in 1945 were a convincing and frightening demonstration of the power of physics. A product of some of the best scientific minds in the world, the nuclear explosions devastated the Japanese cities of Hiroshima and Nagasaki, forcing Japan into an unconditional surrender. But even though the atomic bomb was the most dramatic example, physics and physicists made their presence felt throughout World War II. From dam-breaking bombs that skipped along the water to submerged mines that exploded when they magnetically sensed the presence of a ship's hull, the war was as much a scientific struggle as anything else.

World War II convinced everyone, including skeptical military leaders, that physics is an essential science. Yet the reach of this subject extends far beyond military applications. The principles of physics affect every part of the world and touch on all aspects of people's lives. Hurricanes, lightning, automobile engines, eyeglasses, skyscrapers, footballs, and even the way people walk and run must follow the dictates of scientific laws.

The relevance of physics in everyday life has often been overshadowed by topics such as nuclear weapons or the latest theories of how the universe began. Physics in Our World is a set of volumes that aims to explore the whole spectrum of applications, describing how physics influences technology and society, as well as helping people understand the nature and behavior of the universe and all its many interacting parts. The set covers the major branches of physics and includes the following titles:

- ◆ *Force and Motion*
- ◆ *Electricity and Magnetism*

♦ *Time and Thermodynamics*

♦ *Light and Optics*

♦ *Atoms and Materials*

♦ *Particles and the Universe*

Each volume explains the basic concepts of the subject and then discusses a variety of applications in which these concepts apply. Although physics is a mathematical subject, the focus of these books is on the ideas rather than the mathematics. Only simple equations are included. The reader does not need any special knowledge of mathematics, although an understanding of elementary algebra would be helpful in a few cases. The number of possible topics for each volume is practically limitless, but there is only room for a sample; regrettably, interesting applications had to be omitted. But each volume in the set explores a wide range of material, and all volumes contain a further reading and Web sites section that lists a selection of books and Web sites for continued exploration. This selection is also only a sample, offering suggestions of the many exploration opportunities available.

I was once at a conference in which a young student asked a group of professors whether he needed the latest edition of a physics textbook. One professor replied no, because the principles of physics "have not changed in years." This is true for the most part, but it is a testament to the power of physics. Another testament to physics is the astounding number of applications relying on these principles—and these applications continue to expand and change at an exceptionally rapid pace. Steam engines have yielded to the powerful internal combustion engines of race cars and fighter jets, and telephone wires are in the process of yielding to fiber optics, satellite communication, and cell phones. The goal of these books is to encourage the reader to see the relevance of physics in all directions and in every endeavor, at the present time as well as in the past and in the years to come.

✳ ACKNOWLEDGMENTS ✳

THANKS GO TO my teachers, many of whom did their best to put up with me and my undisciplined ways. Special thanks go to Drs. George Gerstein, Larry Palmer, and Stanley Schmidt for helping me find my way when I got lost. I also much appreciate the contributions of Jodie Rhodes, who helped launch this project; executive editor Frank K. Darmstadt and the editorial and production teams who pushed it along; and the many scientists, educators, and writers who provided some of their time and insight. Thanks most of all go to Elizabeth Kirkland, a super mom with extraordinary powers and a gift for using them wisely.

❋ INTRODUCTION ❋

*F*ORCES COME IN all quantities, from barely noticeable to practically irresistible. A single molecule of air glancing off a person's skin exerts an ignorable force, but together air molecules exert a *pressure,* called atmospheric pressure, which is important in nearly everything people do. And when the wind starts to blow faster than a car on an interstate highway, as it does during a hurricane, forces can reach catastrophic levels.

Forces cause motion, and the study of force and motion is a branch of physics known as mechanics. Motion and force are particularly important in today's mobile society and economy for many reasons. Ships, airplanes, and freight trains haul cargo over long distances; workers commute to and from the office in automobiles or passenger trains; students commute to and from school in buses and automobiles, on bicycles, or by the old-fashioned way of putting one foot in front of the other.

Almost everything moves, and motion can take several forms. An object can move in a straight line, follow a curved pathway, spin around its axis, move back and forth in a periodic way, or make some combination of these movements. Most moving objects on Earth travel through either air or water—substances that have tremendous effects on a pitcher's curveball, a sailor's boat, a diver's submersible, and almost everything else, though often in a less obvious manner than in these examples. Efficiency is important—otherwise transportation would waste precious resources—and safety is even more important. Physics has a lot of principles that apply to both.

Force and Motion looks at forces and motions and how physics, through simple and general concepts, affects the way people live and how the world around them works. No matter what form a movement takes, forces govern the motion. Some of these forces, such as the collision that sends a baseball flying away from a bat, are easy to observe; other forces, such as the one that gives a rocket its thrust, are more difficult to see. But all objects in motion obey laws, whether the object is a wheel or a baseball, a *tsunami* in the ocean or a person walking down the street. The same type of force also turns up in surprisingly distinct places—the force that keeps the space shuttle in its *orbit* is the same as that which gives a block of granite its *weight*.

Objects in motion have *energy*. So does a stretched rubber band or water in an elevated water tank, although this energy is different—it is stored, or potential energy. Storing up energy and converting it into motion is a common way of getting around, and doing this without using up all the world's energy or polluting the environment is another process in which physics is essential.

Each chapter of *Force and Motion* focuses on a single aspect of force and motion. Yet each aspect branches out, covering a wide range of phenomena and relating them in ways unimaginable without the science of physics.

GRAVITY

A N ASTRONAUT FLOATING in space has no sense of up or down. On the surface of Earth, it is the steady downward tug of gravity that provides this sense. Animals and people are so adapted to gravity that this force seems to be a requirement for

Astronaut Bruce McCandless II performed this extravehicular activity in 1984. A backpack with nitrogen jet thrusters provided maneuverability. *(NASA)*

good health: an astronaut's bones and muscles are often significantly weakened after a lengthy stay in orbit.

But gravity's reach extends well beyond the surface of the planet. Sometimes an orbiting astronaut is said to be weightless or in "zero gravity," though this is not accurate. Gravity is still present, although the downward sense of direction is not. Gravity can be subtle, and physicists did not understand this force for a long time. After all, the force that makes an apple fall to the ground on Earth would not necessarily seem to be the same force that holds the solar system together. People believed that the two were different for thousands of years until Sir Isaac Newton (1642–1727) discovered the *universal law of gravitation*.

Because the force of *gravitation* affects what happens not only on this planet but also everywhere else in the universe, it has a tremendous influence on the lives of people here on Earth and on those who venture beyond. Exploration of the solar system, which began in the 1950s, requires a knowledge of gravitational physics, and would not be possible without it. This chapter describes the many ways that the force of gravitation affects people here on Earth, as well as the people who are or will travel into space.

Falling Down

Even before Newton's time, people knew they had to aim a little above a target when using a bow and arrow, or they would miss. The arrow does not follow a straight line to the target but instead curves slightly downward. Gravity affects all things, even swiftly moving arrows. Later, when people began to use even faster projectiles such as cannonballs, it was still necessary to correct for the downward pull of gravity. In the 20th century, as weapons became so powerful that shells could be lobbed for miles, military engineers formulated mathematical tables so that artillery officers could aim their guns with precision. These ballistic tables accounted for not only gravity but also wind, the Earth's rotation, and other factors. To compile these tables before the invention of computers required the efforts of a huge number of mathematically inclined people, and was a very slow process; the need to make ballistic table computations quickly was one of the primary motivations for the development of modern computers.

Newton said that the force of gravitation acts between any two bodies possessing *mass*—which is related to the amount of material a body contains. The reason an arrow, a cannonball, or a dropped key falls to the ground is that there is a strong force of attraction between it and the planet. Since the planet is much bigger than these objects, they are the ones that do almost all the moving. Although the planet is also attracted to them, its movement under such circumstances is insignificant.

Newton discovered that the force due to gravitation between the two masses m_1 and m_2, whose centers are separated by a distance of r, is given by the equation

$$F = (Gm_1m_2) / r^2,$$

in which G is a number called the constant of gravitation. Force is usually described in units called newtons, as described in the sidebar on the next page. Gravitational attraction is proportional to the product of the masses: as either or both of the masses increase, so does the force. But the attraction is inversely proportional to the square of the distance: if the distance is made twice as great, the force is two squared or four times less.

The most important part about Newton's law of gravitation is that it is universal—this law applies to everything in the universe. This includes people, who attract one another in a gravitational sense as well as in an emotional sense. But gravitation is weak compared to other forces. For two average-sized adults standing 3.28 feet (1 m) apart, the gravitational attraction is 0.0000004 newtons—roughly equivalent to the weight of 0.00000009 pounds on the surface of the Earth, which is hardly strong enough to bring together two people who do not like each other's company. For objects that are electrically charged, electrical forces are vastly more powerful than gravity. So are magnetic forces—even a small magnet can hold up objects and defy the force of gravity.

One measure of the strength of Earth's gravity is how fast it can pull down a falling object. Although weak compared to other forces, gravity appears strong on Earth because the planet is so massive.

The Metric System and SI Units

In order to describe the results of measurements, physicists need to use a system of units. Numbers alone are not good enough; to describe a distance as "3" is not useful—is the distance three inches or three miles or three meters? Many people in the United States use the English system of units: foot for distance, pound for weight, and second for time.

The system of units used by most of the world is the *metric system*, a logical system based on factors of 10. The unit of distance is the meter, which can be subdivided into tenths of a meter (decimeter), hundredths (centimeter), thousandths (millimeter), and even smaller amounts. Ten meters is a decameter, 100 is a hectometer, and 1,000 is a kilometer. In terms of the English system of units, one foot is approximately 0.3 meter, and one mile is approximately 1.6 kilometers. The metric unit of mass is the gram. Weight is the force of gravity acting on a mass, and on the surface of Earth a mass of one gram weighs 0.035 ounce. Since this is a small amount, the kilogram (1,000 grams) is often used; a kilogram weighs 2.2 pounds on Earth's surface.

The International System of Units was established in 1960. Called *SI units* (after the French term *Système International*), this system is like the metric system in its use of prefixes such as milli- (thousandth) and kilo- (thousand) to represent quantity.

One can calculate how fast an object should fall because Newton also discovered that the *acceleration* of a mass m_1 due to a force F_1 is F_1/m_1. (This is Newton's second law of motion, to be discussed in more detail in chapter 2.) If a person standing on the surface of the Earth drops a ball of mass m_1, one can determine how fast the ball will fall by writing the force of gravity as F_1 and plugging in the numbers M_E for Earth's mass and R_E for its radius (which is roughly the distance between the center of the ball and the center of Earth):

$$F_1 / m_1 = (Gm_1M_E) / m_1R_E^2 = GM_E / R_E^2.$$

The mass, m_1, of the ball cancels. (This cancellation assumes that the mass experiencing the force of gravitation is the same mass to which Newton's laws of motion apply. This is true as far as physicists have been able to determine.) The most surprising thing

The basis for SI units is a set of specific quantities. The meter, the basic unit of distance, is defined as the distance light travels in 1/299,792,458th of a second. The kilogram, the basic unit of mass, is defined by the mass of a specific platinum-iridium cylinder, carefully maintained and kept at the Bureau International des Poids et Mesures (International Bureau of Weights and Measures) in France. The definition for one second is 9,192,631,770 periods of a particular radiation emitted by cesium atoms. These definitions are required because physicists often make precise measurements, so they have to know the size of the units to an exceptional degree of accuracy. Defining the meter and the second as outlined above means that physicists do not have to rely on a meterstick or an ordinary clock, both of which can be inaccurate. Instead, physicists can produce exactly the standard unit of distance or time in their laboratory. The kilogram has not yet been defined in terms of a physical process, although scientists would like to find one.

The units of other measurements, such as *velocity*, are composed of several basic units. Velocity is distance divided by time—feet per second in English units, meters per second in SI units. The SI unit of force and weight, which is called the newton (N) in honor of Sir Isaac Newton, is equivalent to the product of a kilogram (kg) and meter (m), divided by a second squared (kg·m/s²).

about this is that the rate at which the ball falls, GM_E/R_E^2, does not depend on the ball's mass. This means that everything falls to Earth at the same rate—which, if the values of $G = 6.673 \times 10^{-11}$ Newton·meter²/kilogram², $M_E = 5.98 \times 10^{24}$ kilograms, and $R_E = 3,956$ miles (6,380 km) are used, is approximately 32 feet/second² (9.8 m/s²). In other words, the velocity of a falling object increases by 32 feet/second (9.8 m/s) for every second it falls.

The equation predicts that dropped objects should fall to the ground at the same rate, which is interesting because everyone knows this is not true—objects fall at different rates. When dropped from the same height, a bowling ball will beat a feather to the ground every time, and by quite some distance.

But the equation is not wrong, and the reason why was discovered by the famous physicist Galileo Galilei (1564–1642)—who, coincidentally, died in the same year that Newton was born. Although Galileo was not quite able to derive the equation for gravity, he realized that objects meet resistance from the air as they fall, impeding their motion. When physicists tested Newton's equation by dropping objects in a room in which most of the air had been pumped out, they discovered that the equation was correct. In the absence of air, objects drop at the same rate—the feather and bowling ball land at the same time. If people lived on an airless place like the Moon this would always be obvious, as demonstrated by Apollo astronaut David Scott. While standing on the Moon, he proved the equation correct by letting go of a feather and a hammer at the same height. They hit the surface at exactly the same time.

Sometimes people have imagined what the world would be like if gravity were stronger or weaker than it is. On the Moon objects fall at a slower rate than they do on the Earth, but this is because the Moon has less mass. According to Newton's equation, for two given masses at a certain distance, the strength of the attraction is governed by G, the constant of gravitation. It took a little while for physicists to figure out exactly what value G has—this was finally accomplished by carefully measuring the force of attraction of two known masses at a carefully controlled distance. If G had a different value, the universe would be much different. This could be important because some physicists believe that G may change over time; in other words, G may not be as constant as its name implies. But physicists have not yet found any evidence that this happens. There is also no evidence that people can change G by using a machine or some sort of technology, as imagined by authors such as H. G. Wells, who wrote a story about a spaceship propelled by turning off gravity at the back end of the vessel. Because of this, the ship only felt the Moon's gravity, not Earth's, and the tug of the Moon drew the ship closer. If G could somehow be made to equal zero temporarily, then such "antigravity" devices would be possible, but no one has any idea how to do this.

Physicists know a lot about gravity, thanks to the ideas of Newton, Galileo, and other great scientists. But Newton's discovery of the equation for gravity, useful though it is, does not answer every question about the force of gravitation. A curious person can ask, for example, why two masses attract one another. And why is the force of attraction given by the above equation, and not some other equation? There are as yet no firm answers to these questions, so they will have to await the discoveries of future researchers.

Getting Up

Earth's gravity is what gives people, and other objects, weight. Without gravity, anything not firmly attached to the planet would float away, including the *atmosphere.*

Weight is not the same thing as mass, although the two are related. Weight is the force of gravity acting on an object with mass. An object in space, far away from any planet or star, would have no weight—but it would still have its mass. On the surface of Earth, gravity tugs on objects, making it difficult to lift them up; objects on Earth have weight. Although this keeps things from floating away, gravity also has disadvantages, for on certain occasions it is desirable to get up and go flying off into space, as in the case of the Apollo astronauts. Thanks to gravity, this is extremely difficult.

In trying to get off the planet and into space, a helpful fact is that gravity weakens with the square of the distance, according to Newton's equation. It would be even nicer for astronauts and the National Aeronautics and Space Administration (*NASA*) if the term in the denominator of the equation had a power higher than two, so that gravity would decrease more quickly with distance. But physicists have made careful measurements, and the exponent of the denominator appears to be precisely 2.0.

Distance does matter, though. The Earth is not a perfect sphere—it bulges at the equator—and a person standing at the North Pole or the South Pole is slightly closer to the center of the planet than is a person standing at the equator. A person at one of the poles feels a stronger pull of gravity, and consequently weighs a little more than at the equator. This is a tiny effect, though, because the equator does not bulge very much.

The bad news for the space program is that since Earth is so massive, a person has to be far away from the planet for gravity to become weak. A tremendous amount of energy is required to fight against gravity and lift a ship into space. Such launches require so

A *Delta IV* heavy launch vehicle lifts off from Cape Canaveral, Florida. *(U.S. Air Force/Carleton Bailie)*

much energy that sending ships into space only became possible in the 1950s, about 350 years after Galileo first peered through a telescope and got a close view of the other worlds that could be explored.

How fast does a spaceship have to be going to break free of Earth's gravity? Physicists often use the term *escape velocity*. If an object is traveling as fast as or faster than escape velocity, then it will be able to leave Earth and fly off into space. The escape velocity for Earth is about 6.9 miles/second (11.2 km/s) near the surface of the planet. The velocity is the same for all objects, no matter what their size or mass. This makes sense because all objects also fall at the same rate (not counting air resistance).

To break free of the planet's gravity, astronauts must ride in a vehicle that can reach escape velocity. Whether the vehicle is big or small, the escape velocity is roughly the same, but the size of the vehicle does make a tremendous difference in another way. The less massive an object is, the less energy required to accelerate it; throwing a pebble across a pond is easy—throwing a boulder is not. A huge amount of energy is required to accelerate a big rocket up to escape velocity.

Besides being a difficult problem for NASA, this relationship between mass and acceleration has many other effects. For instance, hydrogen is the lightest atom and can easily reach Earth's escape velocity. This is why there is very little hydrogen in the atmosphere, even though the early atmosphere of Earth contained a lot of it. Hydrogen atoms bounce around, pick up speed due to collisions or heat, and then go off into space. If an astronaut had as little mass as a hydrogen atom, NASA would be very happy.

Real astronauts have considerably more mass than do hydrogen atoms. Accelerating astronauts up to escape velocity means using a powerful rocket. The rocket has to be sturdy so that it can protect the astronauts and withstand the strain of high speed, which means the structure needs a considerable mass. The problem is, therefore, compounded: astronauts as well as a heavy rocket must be accelerated up to escape velocity.

But the problem gets even worse. A powerful rocket engine consumes a great deal of fuel. Fuel has a lot of mass. The list of items that must be accelerated has now grown to include astronauts (and their equipment), the rocket, and the fuel. The fuel burns and is gradually used up, but there must be enough for the ship to reach escape velocity. The more fuel that is needed, the more massive it becomes, and therefore even more fuel is required for acceleration. This is the main reason space travel took so long to develop. It is also the reason why sending ships from Earth to travel throughout the solar system is still quite a rare event today. Even without the astronauts, a rocket and large quantity of fuel is mandatory in order to accelerate equipment such as space probes.

But the situation is not as bad as it could be. Earth is massive, but not as massive or as dense as a lot of objects in the universe. Density is a measure of how much material is in a given volume. A dense planet or other astronomical object packs a lot of mass into a very small radius and has strong gravity as a result. For example, neutron stars (also called pulsars) are billions of times denser than Earth and have a gravitational force billions of times stronger. A marble would weigh more than a million tons (8,900,000,000 N) on a pulsar. Humans could not live there, because the human body would not be strong enough to support its own weight and would collapse instantly.

Orbits and Satellites

Although escape velocity is difficult and expensive to attain, it is fortunately not necessary to do so in many cases. If a spacecraft is launched at a speed that is not quite high enough to allow the craft to reach escape velocity, the craft may go into orbit.

Sir Isaac Newton was one of the first people to understand what an orbit really is. He imagined standing on a mountain and throwing an object such as a rock or an apple. At low velocity the object falls to Earth after traveling a short distance—the act of throwing the object gives it a velocity component parallel to the Earth's surface, but gravity is present and tugs on the object, giving it another velocity component in the downward direction (toward the surface). Velocity is a *vector*, and vectors such as these two velocities combine and determine the direction of travel, as discussed in the following sidebar. Although gravity won the first bout, suppose someone throws the object harder and harder. The

Vectors

Vectors are everywhere in physics. A vector is a quantity having both a magnitude (such as speed) and a direction, and it is distinct from a quantity that has only a magnitude. Mass, for example, has a magnitude—it can be described by a number, such as 4 kilograms or 9 kilograms—but there is no direction associated with the measurement. A quantity that can be described by a single number is known as a *scalar.* Velocity is a vector because it has magnitude and direction. Physicists often draw vectors as arrows, with the orientation representing direction and the length representing magnitude.

Physicists use vectors because nature does—direction is as important as magnitude. A motorist traveling along the highway needs to know not only the speed of the car—50 miles per hour (80 km/hr), say—but also the direction. The car of a traveler wishing to go from St. Louis, Missouri, to Los Angeles, California, should be westbound. The direction determines where the car is going, and the speed determines how fast it will get there. Velocity, being a vector, would in this case be 50 miles per hour (80 km/hr) pointing west.

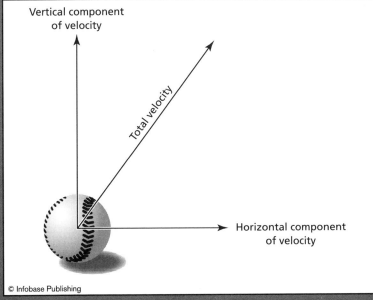

© Infobase Publishing

Any vector can be broken down into its components, such as the horizontal and vertical components of velocity.

object goes farther and farther as its horizontal velocity (parallel to the surface) increases, until finally, Newton realized, it would be going so fast that it would travel all the way around the world.

An object is said to orbit a planet or a star if it is going fast enough to keep from falling to the surface, but not quite fast enough to break away from gravity's grip. Earth is a planet in the solar system and is in orbit around the Sun, and the Moon is a *satellite* of Earth and is in orbit around the planet. A large number of small machines called artificial satellites (usually just referred to as satellites) also orbit Earth.

Once a body gets into an orbit, it needs no engine or fuel to stay there. The Moon certainly has no engines, and the artificial satellites in orbit around the Earth generally have weak engines, which fire only so often and have nothing to do with keeping the machine from falling. There is nothing to keep an orbiting satellite from falling, and this is precisely what happens—it falls all the time. That is what an orbit is.

An orbiting object continually falls toward the planet or star or whatever it is orbiting. The only reason the object fails to land is that it is going at just the right speed so that it continually misses the surface. The many communications satellites orbiting Earth, for example, are all going at a high rate of speed—slower than escape velocity but still fast. They have not escaped Earth's gravitational field, which keeps tugging on them; gravity is the reason they stick around. Orbiting objects are in "free fall"—they are in the same situation as a stone falling to the ground—but unlike a stone, they maintain their altitude because of their velocity. They continually travel around Earth, falling but never landing.

The effects of free fall are evident on astronauts who are in orbiting spacecraft, such as a space shuttle. They float around the ship, as does everything else that is not fastened down. There seems to be no gravity, which is why this effect is sometimes called *weightlessness* or *zero gravity*. But these are inappropriate names. Gravity is very much present—an orbit is impossible without it. The space shuttle commonly orbits at an altitude of 184 miles (296 km) above Earth's surface, and gravity is only 5 percent weaker than it is at sea level, a barely noticeable difference.

Astronauts float about the cabin of a space shuttle not because they are in the absence of gravity but because they are in orbit, and thus in free fall. Like their ship, they are continually falling; but also like their ship, they are going fast enough to stay in orbit. Since a space shuttle and everything aboard it are in free fall, things that are "dropped" in the orbiting ship do not fall to the floor, but instead float around the cabin. This is because the ship and everything in it are falling right along with the "dropped" object.

The free-fall nature of orbits is of crucial importance to today's society. Without orbits, a lot of useful things such as telecommunications and satellite-television broadcasts would be so expensive as to be practically unaffordable. An orbiting satellite is not going as fast as escape velocity but it does have to be going quite fast, and a huge amount of energy is required to reach that speed. But—and this is the good part—because an orbit is simply a free fall, the satellite does not require any fuel once the orbital speed is reached. Satellites do not need engines or fuel to stay in orbit once they get there. (They are in free fall, which needs no fuel. However, they do require an engine if they are to have the ability to change their orbit.)

There is one other practical requirement: all orbits have to be above a certain altitude, above the planet's atmosphere. Otherwise the air would hit a satellite and cause a "drag" that would decrease the speed and send it plummeting to Earth. Although the atmosphere thins out slowly and there is no abrupt end, there is little air above 62 miles (100 km). (Most long-term satellites orbit at considerably higher altitudes, because even a small amount of air will cause enough drag to bring them down.) It would be possible, of course, to keep an object circling Earth below this altitude, but a tremendous amount of energy would be required to overcome the air resistance. Once an object is in orbit above the atmosphere it does not require fuel to stay there, which is why orbits are so beneficial.

Even though people often say that Earth circles the Sun and a satellite circles Earth, orbits are not exactly circular but elliptical (oval). But in many cases orbits are very close to being circular.

Centuries ago physicists studied orbits to understand how the solar system works and found that not only are orbits elliptical—which surprised them, as they had assumed orbits would be circular—but also that there is a relationship between the period of an orbiting object and its altitude. The farther away an orbiting body is, the slower it moves. This is often stated as one of Kepler's laws (named after Johannes Kepler [1571–1630], the German astronomer who first discovered it), but it turns out simply to be a consequence of the universal law of gravitation. This is extremely important, particularly when people first began to put objects into orbit around Earth. The period of an orbit—the time required for one complete revolution—depends on altitude. For example, for an approximately circular orbit at an altitude of 184 miles (296 km), the orbital period is close to one hour and thirty minutes. This is a common orbit of a space shuttle—every one and a half hours, space shuttle astronauts complete one trip around the globe.

Higher orbits have longer periods. At 6,200 miles (10,000 km), the orbital period is about five hours and 45 minutes. At 62,000 miles (100,000 km), the period is nearly four days; at this distance, it would take four days to make one revolution. Meanwhile, of course, Earth is spinning below—in this case, faster than the satellite is revolving, since Earth makes a complete revolution in one day. Because objects orbiting at a given altitude have a certain period and therefore travel at a certain velocity, in order for people to place a satellite at that altitude it has to be traveling at the required velocity. For example, the velocity for an approximately circular orbit at 184 miles (296 km) is 17,270 miles/hour (7,720 m/s).

Once people understood the physics of orbits, putting satellites in orbit became possible (after rockets with sufficient power were built). The first successful artificial satellite was *Sputnik 1*, launched in October 1957 by the Soviet Union. Many historians consider this momentous event to mark the beginning of a new era—the Space Age.

Satellites are crucial for a lot of the things people take for granted today—things that were impossible before 1957. Satellites orbiting at high altitudes get better than even a bird's-eye view of the world. Weather measurements and forecasting, for example, have been vastly improved by satellite observations. But perhaps the most commonplace use of satellites is in communications.

Before satellites, communication with radio waves and other electromagnetic waves was limited. Unlike sound waves, which bend around corners, radio waves generally travel in a straight line. A person's voice can be heard even if he or she is not in sight, but a receiver for electromagnetic waves usually needs to be in or close to the line of sight of the transmitter in order to get good reception. Broadcasters such as radio and television stations build tall towers so that the signals travel to as large a reception area as possible. There are certain exceptions to this—sometimes radio signals bounce off a layer of the atmosphere called the ionosphere (which is why radios can occasionally receive distant stations, especially at night). But before satellites, the only reliable way to get around the limitations of electromagnetic waves was to lay expensive cables, which carry signals in the form of electrical pulses.

It occurred to scientists and engineers that using satellites would be a good way to transmit radio signals. If the satellite has a high orbit, it can be in the line of sight of a huge reception area. In effect, the satellite is like an extremely tall tower. The signals could be sent to the satellite, which would beam them to receivers. A satellite called *Telstar 1* relayed the first transatlantic television broadcast in 1962; viewers all the way across the Atlantic Ocean could watch the shows.

But there is a problem. Satellites move and Earth spins, which means that, unlike a tower that is firmly attached to the ground, most satellites do not stay over one spot. Relaying communication signals is tricky, for the line of sight and the reception area are always changing.

Fortunately, a simple solution to this problem exists. Science fiction author Arthur C. Clarke suggested the solution all the way back in the 1940s, before there was even such a thing as an artificial satellite. The solution makes use of two facts: the orbital period of a satellite depends on altitude, and Earth rotates within a period of 24 hours. To get a satellite to hover over one spot, it is simply necessary to find the altitude at which the orbital period is 24 hours. The motion of the satellite at this altitude matches the rotation of the Earth. Such an orbit is called a *geosynchronous orbit*. The altitude is 22,250 miles (35,780 km) and is extremely important for many types of telecommunications, such as satellite television. But there is a limitation: geosynchronous orbits are possible only over the equator, because only over the equator will the path of the orbit keep in step with the rotating Earth. This does not present too many difficulties, although it does limit the number of satellites that can be in geosynchronous orbit at any one time.

Another common application of satellites is their use in navigation. Sailors in the open sea have long had to depend on various and not always reliable means to find their location. Pinpointing one's location on land is also frequently essential. The ability to do this with tremendous accuracy became available with the development of the Global Positioning System (GPS), which uses a set of 24 satellites. The satellites are not in geosynchronous orbit (their altitude is quite a bit lower), but they were specifically placed in orbits where at least four satellites are over every point on the Earth at any given time. The satellites continually transmit signals that can be picked up by anyone with a GPS receiver; the signals contain the satellite coordinates and time information that allow the receiver to calculate its location automatically on the surface of the Earth within a few feet.

Many ships use GPS, and even some automobiles take advantage of the technology. GPS is also indispensable in many engineering projects. The tunnel under the English Channel linking England with France (known as the Chunnel) was carved out by large tunnel-borers working on both sides of the English Channel. But how did they manage to meet in the middle and not miss one another? GPS provided their coordinates so that they stayed on track and avoided an expensive mistake.

The physics of orbits is critical for reasons other than just modern technology. Physicists and astronomers have used their knowledge of orbits to learn much about the solar system as well as the rest of the universe.

The universal law of gravitation says that all objects attract each other. But when a small artificial satellite or even a space shuttle orbits Earth, the large planet seems to be unaffected. This is for the most part true, but since gravity is a two-way affair, Earth is attracted to the satellites. Orbiting objects are always revolving about some point between the centers of the two objects. This can be seen more easily when considering the orbit of a large object such as the Moon. Although people often say that the Moon orbits Earth, the reality is that both the Moon and Earth orbit a common point between them. But because Earth is 80 times more massive than the Moon, that point is much closer to the center of Earth and is even within Earth itself, though not the center. For much smaller satellites, the common point is not significantly different from Earth's center.

But for large objects, there can be definite effects of gravity on the motion of the bodies they orbit. The Sun is much larger than all the planets combined, yet the combined mass of the planets is sufficient to cause a small wobble in the motion of the Sun as it travels through the galaxy. This is true for any other star with a lot of orbiting planets, and if the wobble is large enough it can be detected by astronomers using sensitive instruments. This is how the first planets known to exist outside the solar system were discovered.

The existence of large orbiting objects can also have an effect on other objects that are orbiting the same body. Massive satellites can cause the orbit of other objects to be perturbed, or, in other words, to depart from the motion, as calculated by the law of gravitation, that would be expected if the perturbing object was not present. If an object's orbit is perturbed, the existence of some other massive object is evident, and its location can sometimes even be determined. This is exactly how astronomers Urbain-Jean-Joseph Le Verrier and John Couch Adams predicted the existence of the planet Neptune, which was found in 1846: its gravity was affecting the orbit of nearby Uranus.

The Apollo Adventure: Going to the Moon

One of the greatest achievements made possible by an understanding of gravity is space exploration. There have always been people who love to explore. Whether it is the next town, the countryside beyond the hill, or continents far across the ocean, a few daring men and women are willing to endure hardship and risk to go there. This is even true for the trip to the Moon, which is about 248,000 miles (400,000 km) away.

But leaving Earth requires achieving escape velocity. As discussed earlier, the amount of energy needed depends on the mass of the object to be accelerated. Manned missions to the Moon required accelerating astronauts plus their equipment and supplies. This is the kind of job for a huge, powerful rocket, along with a lot of fuel, which added even more to the burden.

The mission was only possible after the construction of the gigantic rocket called the Saturn V (pronounced "saturn five"—V is the Roman numeral for five). This rocket, standing 363 feet (110.6 m) tall, had such large engines that when they were turned on they would cause miniature earthquakes for miles around. The engines were extremely powerful, generating millions of horsepower (the average car today has about 180 horsepower). The engines were also dangerous, because if something went wrong they could explode in a horrific fireball.

The Saturn V rocket solved the problem of reaching escape velocity, so the astronauts could leave the Earth. But there was another problem—finding and hitting the target, the Moon. Physics is often called a precise science, and in this case it really had to be, because this was not an easy problem. The Russians launched the first unmanned probe toward the Moon in 1959. The Russian scientists were smart and experienced, and the probe, called *Luna 1,* came quite near to the target. *Luna 1* was only off by a few thousand miles, which is a small error considering the size of the solar system. But it was not quite good enough. The probe failed to land on the Moon and went right on going, captured by the Sun's immense gravity. The Russian news agency described the incident with the best possible spin: they announced that their country was the first to put a probe into orbit around the Sun.

Launching a rocket that will actually reach the Moon requires an understanding of gravity and a lot of calculations. Back in the 1950s and 1960s, computers were not nearly as powerful as they are today, so finding the solution took a great deal of time. This was a case where the physics was understood, but the difficulty

The Saturn V rocket launched the Apollo 11 mission on July 16, 1969, from Kennedy Space Center. *(NASA)*

was in achieving the required precision. Scientists and engineers gradually solved the problem, and both Russia and the United States were able to launch unmanned probes that managed to land on the Moon.

The Apollo Project, conducted by the United States in the 1960s and early 1970s, consisted of a number of missions, each mission being given a consecutive number. The early Apollo missions tested the equipment and the procedures that would be used to reach the Moon. On July 16, 1969, three astronauts of *Apollo 11* (the 11th Apollo mission)—Neil Armstrong, Buzz Aldrin, and Michael Collins—rode the 800-foot (244-m) flame of a Saturn V rocket on a successful liftoff from Cape Canaveral, Florida, and headed east, the first of several Apollo missions intended to land on the Moon.

But why Florida? Physics provides the answer. The east coast of Florida was the launch point for several good reasons. One of the most important reasons is that it has a low latitude—meaning it is closer to the equator than is most of the rest of the United States. This is critical because Earth is a sphere and spins on its axis, and the speed of rotation depends on latitude. At the North Pole and the South Pole the speed is zero, since these points lie on the axis of rotation. The rotation speed at the equator—the lowest latitude—is the greatest. This same effect can be seen with a spinning basketball: a point near the top of the ball is going round and round slowly, and a point near the middle is moving much more quickly.

This matters because a lot of energy must be expended to reach escape velocity, and every little extra boost counts. By launching at a low latitude and heading east (in the direction of Earth's spin), rockets take advantage of Earth's rotational velocity. It is a little push forward, provided by the planet's rotation.

Mission planners also had to consider the possibility of a tragic accident. Launching big rockets, particularly in the 1960s, was a risky endeavor. The east coast of Florida was a good location because the rocket headed east, taking it at once out over the ocean. Any disaster would have occurred over the ocean instead of over populated land, where even more people could have gotten hurt by falling debris.

After the successful launch, the engines of the Saturn V eventually exhausted their fuel. Once the fuel was gone, the rocket jettisoned these engines to reduce weight. The rocket kept going forward because in the vacuum of space there is little air to resist motion. Only a small part of the rocket remained, which was the spacecraft containing the astronauts and their supplies.

While traveling to the Moon, the astronauts were busy but were also able to get some rest. The hard job had been launching the rocket and aiming it so that the mission would reach the Moon. Although the astronauts made some course corrections by firing a small jet to maneuver the spaceship, they were mostly content to relax and let "Sir Isaac Newton do the driving." In other words, they recognized that the knowledge physicists have of the force of gravitation was good enough to get them safely to their destination.

The astronauts went into orbit around the Moon after they reached their destination four days later. A small module of the craft detached and carried two astronauts, Neil Armstrong and Buzz Aldrin, to the surface of the Moon. Michael Collins maintained orbit, waiting for his two colleagues to return. On July 20, 1969, Neil Armstrong became the first person to step on the Moon. Armstrong and Aldrin spent several hours on the surface and then lifted off to rejoin Collins and return to Earth. Liftoff from the Moon was much easier than from Earth because the Moon is so much smaller and less massive. The Moon's gravity is only one-sixth as strong as Earth's, so Armstrong and Aldrin did not need the huge engines of a Saturn V rocket. All three astronauts arrived back on Earth safely on July 24, 1969.

As Armstrong took the first step on the Moon, he said, "That's one small step for a man, one giant leap for mankind." It was a leap accomplished by the courage and resourcefulness of the astronauts who went on the journey, the skill and intelligence of the engineers who designed the equipment, and the knowledge of the physicists who made it all possible.

Navigating in the Solar System

The Moon landings were a tremendous accomplishment, but the space program did not stop there. Although there have not been any manned missions beyond the Moon, plenty of unmanned spaceships have traveled throughout the solar system.

Navigating in space is a lot different in reality from how it is portrayed on television and in the movies. Fictional spaceships often take a direct route from one planet to the next, traveling in straight lines. In these stories, navigation is a matter of plotting a course—as a ship's crew would on the ocean—and then firing up the engines. This makes sense in science fiction, but it is not an accurate description of how manned and unmanned ships presently travel through space. Traveling in a straight shot from one place to another in the solar system may seem like the best way to go—and it is certainly the shortest distance—but it is not feasible at the present time. The reason is due to gravity.

When a ship attains escape velocity and leaves Earth, this is not the end of the force of gravitation on that ship. There is also the Sun, which is 330,000 times more massive than Earth; because of its strong gravity, the Sun affects the motion of everything traveling in our solar system.

Earth, like the rest of the planets, orbits the Sun, in the same way the Moon and the artificial satellites orbit Earth. When a spaceship manages to escape Earth, it is still very much within the gravitational influence of the Sun. (Recall the fate of Russian probe *Luna 1*.) This was not a big problem for the Moon missions, for the Moon is, in terms of the immense size of the solar system, just next door. But when astronauts wish to travel to, say, Mars—whose elliptical orbit is 34–62 million miles (55–100 million km) away—this is a big problem. It is a bigger problem when other planets, which are even farther away, are the desired destinations.

To fight gravity by traveling against the pull of the Sun requires a tremendous amount of energy, as it does to travel against Earth's gravity. The problem is the same as before. This energy must be provided by the combustion of fuel, which has a lot of mass. But the worse thing is that spaceships would have to carry this extra fuel with them as they lift off from Earth. The fuel would add considerable mass, making the launch much more expensive. Extremely powerful engines are necessary, which means liftoffs would also be much more dangerous.

Cheap and practical space travel demands that this dilemma be avoided. The solution is identical to the approach people take with satellites—make use of orbits.

Traveling against gravity requires a great deal of effort, but traveling with, instead of against, gravity does not—riding a bicycle downhill is always easier than pedaling uphill. Because an orbit is a free fall, space probes and spaceships mostly travel in the solar system just as the planets do. The ship or probe achieves an orbit and "falls" to the desired location. The launch still requires energy to lift off from Earth and maneuver into an orbit around the Sun, but once the ship attains its orbit, it needs to make only minor corrections and requires only a little fuel to maintain the proper course. This is obviously not the fastest way to reach a given destination—the fastest (and shortest) way is a straight line, rather than a roundabout orbit—but a straight line would require a fight against gravitation.

To send a probe to Jupiter, for example, the ship must be boosted into an orbit around the Sun that at some point will intersect the orbit of Jupiter. Careful planning is essential, because Jupiter has to be exactly at that point in its orbit when the ship arrives. The job would be completely impossible without an understanding of the dynamics of the solar system, which means, of course, an understanding of the force of gravitation.

There is another way to use gravity while traveling throughout the solar system. Many space probes, such as *Voyager* and *Galileo*, have utilized a method called gravity assist.

Gravity assists occur when a probe passes close to a planet or other large body in the solar system. Unless it has been deliberately aimed for the planet, the probe is usually traveling too fast to go into orbit; as described earlier, orbits are strongly related to velocities, and anything traveling too fast for a given planet will not be captured by its gravity (unless the object is traveling on a course that makes a direct hit on the planet—something generally to be avoided). However, as the probe passes close to the planet, it does come under the influence of the planet's gravity. The effect—if the probe is going in the right direction—is an increase in probe speed, as illustrated in the figure on page 24.

The increase in speed is due to a kind of slingshot effect. The planet is orbiting the Sun with a certain orbital velocity, and the probe, traveling at its own speed, flies by. The planet's gravity tugs at the probe, and if the probe is moving in the same direction as the planet, the probe whips forward. The effect is similar to that of

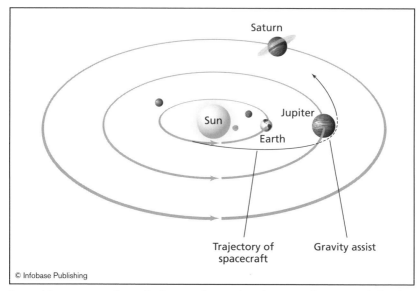

Spaceships get a gravity assist from a planet when it comes close enough for the planet's gravity to influence its trajectory.

a conveyor belt. If a walking person steps onto a moving conveyor belt, his or her speed becomes the original walking speed plus the speed of the belt. The boost in speed of the probe does not come free, because the planet slows down slightly, but since the planet is so massive, the amount of slowdown is negligible.

The opposite effect works too and has also been done frequently. If the probe flies by in the direction opposite the planet's orbital velocity, the probe slows down (and the planet speeds up, although by an extremely small and undetectable amount).

Why would anyone want to slow a space probe? The reason is to change its orbit. An orbiting object is in free fall, so it needs to derive no energy from fuel in order to move in its orbit; but to change its orbit, the object must have fuel. This is because changing an object's orbit means changing its velocity; the object must either speed up or slow down. In space, a change in velocity requires the use of rocket propellant—squirting some gas out of a nozzle in a backward direction speeds up the ship, and squirting some out the front slows it down. But in order to have this propellant available the ship must have lifted off from Earth with the propellant on board. Propellant is heavy—the liftoff problem again. To avoid this problem, yet maintain the probe's ability to maneuver and navigate in the solar system, scientists and engineers try to use other means to change the probe's velocity. Often, this means using gravity—like the gravity assist method.

Humans have only just begun to explore the vastness of the universe. The force of gravitation holds together the stars, planets, and galaxies, and is also the force that binds people to the planet Earth—the force that must be conquered whenever astronauts wish to leave Earth. The first few journeys beyond this planet have so far been baby steps in the immensity of space. But these trips are a good beginning—a beginning in which physics has been and will continue to be essential.

2
LINEAR MOVEMENT

WHY DOES ESCAPING Earth's gravity take a lot of effort? A hydrogen atom hardly needs any push at all to fly off into space, but a rocket carrying astronauts and loaded with fuel would fail to achieve escape velocity without a tremendous thrust.

Crucial relationships exist for the quantities of force, mass, and motion. All moving bodies obey these relationships, from rockets in space to cars on the highway—everything that moves. An understanding of the physics of force and motion is essential to today's society because of the heavy reliance on transportation: the economy of most countries in the world depends on safe, efficient means of transporting passengers and cargo. There is also a great need to predict the path of moving objects or systems of objects. Perhaps the most surprising thing is that are limits on the ability of science to make predictions. But for the most part physics describes motion with phenomenal accuracy, provided one understands the concept called *inertia*.

Inertia

Before the time of Galileo, people thought that things move only if they are pushed or pulled. This makes sense because a cart moves only if someone or something pushes or pulls it (except for rolling downhill—but the cart will eventually stop when it reaches level ground). Unpowered objects tend to come to a stop. People incorrectly believed that pushing an object with a constant force meant that the object traveled at a constant velocity.

But Galileo realized that a force—a push or a pull—does not make things go at a constant velocity. The consequence of a force acting on a body is not constant velocity but rather a change in its velocity. To explain this, Galileo came up with the idea of inertia. Inertia is a resistance to a change in motion and is measured in terms of an object's mass. A change in motion means any change whatsoever—it can mean a change from standing still to being in motion, or from being in motion to standing still, or a change in how fast the object is moving, or even just a change in direction.

Inertia means that objects at rest tend to stay at rest, and objects in motion tend to stay in motion. People must always consider inertia as they move around, throw something, or calculate the motion of other objects, but everyone forgets about inertia once in a while. When inexperienced basketball players run toward the basket and shoot the ball for a layup, they often shoot too hard and miss. These players throw the ball toward the hoop, but the ball is already moving in this direction because it is traveling with the player. The ball does not usually require any extra push forward since it will continue its motion toward the hoop after it is released—the ball has inertia. If the player is moving quickly, all that is needed is to toss the ball upward, not forward. With a correctly timed release, the ball will make an arching trajectory into the basket.

Inertia is also important in football. Defensive players want to rush behind the line of scrimmage and tackle the quarterback, and offensive linemen must block them. On most football teams, offensive linemen are the biggest, most massive players. Their mass gives them a lot of inertia, making it difficult for the defensive players to push them out of the way.

Because of inertia, an object's motion does not change without application of a force. The mathematical equations and laws describing motion in terms of forces were developed by Sir Isaac Newton—a physicist who, like Galileo, spent a great deal of his time discovering new concepts. Newton came up with these laws

Basketballs obey the laws of motion, as does every other object. This Air Force Academy forward scores two points. *(U.S. Air Force/David Armer)*

about 300 years ago but they are still important in just about everything people do. The sidebar on page 29 describes Newton's first and second laws.

Newton's First and Second Laws

Newton's first law of motion is a restatement of Galileo's idea of inertia; it says that an object that is not being acted upon by any force will travel at a constant velocity. (The velocity could be zero, which means that an object at rest tends to stay at rest.)

Newton's second law of motion relates a force (F), acceleration (a), and mass m in a remarkably general and often used equation. In its most simplified form, the equation is $F = ma$.

A force acting on a body equals the body's mass multiplied by its acceleration. Acceleration refers to a change in velocity, as shown in the figure. Both acceleration and force are vector quantities—they have magnitude and direction. Mass, being a scalar, does not have a direction. The equation implies that the direction of the acceleration vector is equal to the direction of the force vector, which makes sense. An object accelerates in the direction in which it is pushed or pulled. When there is more than one force, solving the equation requires calculation of the sum of the forces.

A slightly more complicated form of Newton's second law involves a quantity called *linear momentum*, which is equal to mass multiplied by velocity. In this form, the law states that force equals a change in momentum. The change could be either in mass or in velocity—but since mass does not often change, the equation is usually written using the product of mass and acceleration (the change in velocity), as above.

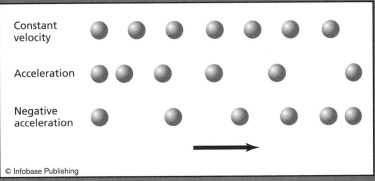

© Infobase Publishing

The distance a ball travels in a one-second interval is the same when its velocity is constant but gets larger or smaller as it accelerates.

Sometimes forces are not easy to detect, which is the reason the concepts of inertia and forces did not become well understood before Galileo and Newton. A moving cart slows and stops when it is no longer pushed because of several forces. When things move or rub against each other—such as a cart's wheel rubbing against its axle—this acts as a force, called *friction,* which will reduce speed. Another force acting on the cart is air resistance. As the cart moves, air pushes against it, slowing it down.

Catching a Ride

Friction and air resistance become even more important at the faster speeds with which people travel these days. The force exerted by air is usually proportional to the square of the object's speed—if the speed is doubled, air resistance rises fourfold. In the 1970s, when there was a sharp reduction in gasoline supplies, the government lowered the speed limit on American highways from 70 miles per hour (112 km/hr) to 55 miles per hour (88 km/hr). The reduced speed meant much lower air resistance, which reduced the amount of gasoline needed to power the automobiles.

The boxy front end of an older car (center) encounters more air resistance than do the sleek front ends of the newer cars parked nearby. *(Kyle Kirkland)*

(Reduced speed also tends to decrease the severity of accidents.) Many people are fond of going fast, though, and speed limits have since been raised in most states.

Objects with mass have inertia, and when they are not subject to friction or air resistance—for instance, in space, far away from Earth's atmosphere—they will move at a constant velocity. As Galileo said, a change requires a force. A force can also offset another force (such as air resistance or friction) in order to prevent that force from making a change. A cart or a wagon needs a push or pull so that friction and air resistance will not bring it to a halt. To accelerate an object, enough force must be applied to offset friction and air resistance plus at least a little more beyond that amount; the extra portion will accelerate the object at a rate given by Newton's second law.

Cars with powerful engines can accelerate quickly. Acceleration is, in fact, the only time when automobile engines must exert a large force; when a car cruises down the highway at a constant speed, the engine does not need much activity to offset friction and air resistance. But a large (quick) acceleration will only happen with the application of a large force—according to Newton's second law—and this is why manufacturers test their high-performance automobiles by measuring the time required to accelerate from 0 to 60 miles per hour (96 km/hr). The Lamborghini Diablo, an expensive car with an enormously powerful engine, can go from 0 to 60 miles per hour in less than four seconds. (Such tests can only be correctly and safely done under certain conditions and on a special track.) Motorcycles, being less massive than cars, do not need as powerful an engine to accelerate. Less mass means less inertia.

Newton's laws say that when acceleration is zero, so is the net force. (In other words, the sum of the forces acting on the object must add to zero.) This is the reason objects falling through the air to the ground reach what is called a terminal velocity. Gravity causes unsupported objects to accelerate toward the ground, but the faster they go, the stronger air resistance becomes, until finally the drag produced by air resistance equals the force of gravity. At this point there is no net force and therefore no more acceleration—the object has reached terminal velocity, the value of which depends on the shape of the object (because the shape affects air resistance). Terminal velocity for a falling person with arms and legs extended is about 120 miles per hour (192 km/hr), but when curled up in a ball, a person can fall a little bit quicker because the air resistance is decreased.

Slowing Down

Thanks to inertia, an object experiencing no net force will not change its motion; specifically, it will not slow down and come to a halt if it is moving. Coming to a halt requires a force, the effects of which can be quite a learning experience. Late in the 19th century the first "horseless carriages"—now known as cars—began appearing. These early cars gave many riders an excellent though somewhat unfortunate demonstration of Newton's laws of motion.

Unlike horses—which have good eyesight and a lot of common sense—cars had a habit of running into things and suddenly crashing to a stop (especially when steered by an inexperienced driver). The driver, however, in a painful demonstration of inertia, kept going, usually tumbling over the windscreen of these open-roofed vehicles. Speeds were low at the time, so the driver and any passengers would likely escape with just dusty clothes and some bumps and bruises. But as cars became faster, sudden stops became increasingly jarring. The need for seat belts became apparent.

Slowing down is just a special case of acceleration. Some people call it deceleration, but physicists tend to use the term *negative acceleration*. The most important thing about slowing down is how fast it is done. A very slow and gradual stop is hardly noticeable, but a sudden one is.

A change in momentum in either direction—speeding up or slowing down—requires a force. The more massive an object is, the harder it is to stop. This is clear from Newton's second law, $F = ma$, which can be written as $a = F/m$; when the mass, m, is great, the change in velocity, a, is small for a given force, F. This fact is particularly evident in trains. In the early 19th century, when trains were first built, few trains had brakes because nobody knew a safe and effective way to stop something so massive. Instead of braking, trains simply coasted to a stop. In case of an emergency, the engineer might try to bring the locomotive to a halt by reversing the engine, but this was not a safe option; several trains derailed during such attempts.

Engineers could not safely bring trains to a stop until the development of air brakes by American businessman George Westinghouse in the 1860s. Air brakes use high-pressure air to push something hard against the wheels to increase friction. Even so, trains continue to need a huge amount of time and distance to brake—long freight trains often take more than a mile to stop. Getting in front of a train is always dangerous because so much force is needed to change its momentum, and this cannot be done quickly.

Mass is important in slowing down, but so is speed. The faster something is going, the harder it is to stop. This is also a consequence of Newton's laws. Airplanes must go very fast in order to stay in the air, but landing is tricky. When an airplane touches down, it has so much speed that its wheel brakes might fail if pilots use them; instead, pilots apply other methods to slow down, such as reversing the thrust of the engines and using air resistance created by raising the wing flaps. A big airplane's brakes are usually effective only when the speed has been significantly reduced.

Critical in all this is the fact that any force acts over a certain period of time. The quantity that equals force multiplied by time is *impulse,* and it is important in terms of momentum. A force changes momentum—Newton's second law—and changing momentum by a large amount takes either a large force acting over a short time, or a small force acting over a long time. An object gets momentum—mass multiplied by velocity—from an impulse. The term *linear momentum* refers to momentum of an object traveling in a straight line, as opposed to rotational or *angular momentum* (the subject of the following chapter).

Momentum is a conserved quantity, and it is an extremely important consideration when analyzing collisions. Consider the impact of a moving billiard ball when it smacks into another ball that is initially at rest. As the first ball hits the second one and imparts a significant force, the second ball receives an impulse; although the force acts only for a short period of time (the collision), the impulse is usually enough to get the second ball rolling.

Another way of saying this is that the first ball transfers some or all of its momentum to the second. If it gives away all its momentum, the first ball simply stops, and the momentum of the second ball equals the moment of the first ball before the collision. If the collision results in only a partial transfer of the momentum, then the sum of the momenta (plural of *momentum*) of the two moving balls must equal the first ball's original momentum.

The amount of time that a force acts is critical in safety devices. When a car crashes into a wall at 40 miles per hour (64 km/hr), the momentum of the car—and, more important, the passengers—goes from a high value down to zero. (The momentum does not disappear; the collision transfers the momentum to another object, as mentioned in the billiard ball example above. If the other object is massive—say, a brick wall firmly attached to Earth—then the object does not pick up much velocity in the exchange. If for a given momentum the mass, m, is large, the velocity, v, is going to be small.) The main problem for the people riding in the car during a collision is that the impulse consists of an extremely large force acting over a very short time.

Seat belts are necessary because they prevent inertia from sending passengers through a windshield. But also needed is a reduction in the force experienced by passengers; small forces can be endured safely but large forces cause injuries. This is where air bags come in. Air bags work by reducing the force, and they do this by making the impulse act over a longer period of time. The change in momentum is the same—the car and riders come to a stop—but the riders come to a stop over a longer period of time, because of a cushion of air. This is the same reason why a falling person would much rather land on a pile of leaves than on a patch of hard ground. As time increases, force decreases.

Reducing the force makes a big difference. A gunner in World War II once bailed out of a burning bomber flying at 18,000 feet (5.5 km) without a parachute. He reached terminal velocity but miraculously survived, because his momentum did not change in-stantly but instead was gradually reduced by a series of minor impacts with some tree branches and then a large quantity of snow.

Air bags have been mandatory in cars since 1997. They are activated by a sudden change in the car's momentum caused by a

This car's air bags have been activated due to a collision. The air eventually escapes, so the air bags become flat. *(Kyle Kirkland)*

powerful force. This is crucial to the activation process, which is why using the car's brakes will not engage the air bag. In most cars, the maximum braking force is only about 10 percent as strong as what is required to activate the air bags.

Although air bags act to reduce the force experienced by the rider by making his or her change of momentum occur over a longer period of time, they can be hazardous if the rider hits the air bag at an awkward angle. Wearing seat belts is still necessary and helps position the rider for a safe "landing" in case of an accident.

Nature also uses the same concept that makes air bags work. There is a type of hedgehog in Europe that is fond of climbing trees. The animal is not so good at getting back down again (rather like certain cats). But these hedgehogs have an array of needles, similar to those of a porcupine, and the animals put them to excellent use in such situations. A treed hedgehog simply rolls up into a ball and falls to the ground. The needles are flexible and bend on impact, which brings the animal to a relatively slow stop. This reduces the force so that the fall does not injure the hedgehog. Cats, on the other hand, require rescuing by someone with a tall ladder and considerable patience.

Unpredictable Movement: Chaos

Newton's equations of motion are simple and precise. They permit calculation of a body's trajectory well in advance if the forces acting on it are known. This is particularly important in calculating the trajectory of asteroids in the solar system, because of the potential danger they present if one of them should strike Earth.

But sometimes the equations used by physicists are not simple, and they may be difficult to solve. Even Newton's equations of motion become complicated if the forces are complex, or if there are a lot of objects and forces to be considered. In such cases, fast and expensive computers are necessary to do the calculations. Supercomputers are astonishingly fast computers with a large number of computer chips called microprocessors that perform a huge number of calculations each second. The computer called Deep Blue, which beat champion Garry Kasparov in chess in 1997, is an example.

People often want to calculate the trajectory of a body or the motion of a system of bodies over a long period of time, which enables a prediction of the system's behavior for a long time in the future. Will an approaching asteroid hit Earth? To give people time to do something to prevent the disaster, warning of the asteroid must come while it is still far away. Also important is tracking the movement of severe weather systems, in order to provide advance warning to people in the path.

Unfortunately, scientists recently discovered that in certain situations accurate predictions are possible only for a short period of time. Physicists can predict the path of an asteroid over the course of years (not perfectly but with excellent accuracy), but meteorologists cannot accurately predict the weather more than a few days or so in the future. This is because weather is an example of a system that exhibits *chaos*.

Chaos, as physicists use the term, does not refer to something having no order. Chaos refers to specific mathematical properties of certain types of equation. When the motion of a system is governed by equations that have the mathematical properties of chaos, it is generally impossible to predict the system's long-range behavior. These equations are usually complex and always nonlinear, which means they cannot be visualized in a graph as straight lines.

Understanding chaos requires an understanding of *dynamical systems,* which are objects or systems of objects that change over time. To plot the future movement of a dynamical system, it is necessary to know the equations of motion and the state of the system at a given moment. In other words, if physicists know the condition (state) of a system at a specific moment in time, and they also know how the system will evolve (the equations of motion), they can predict its future behavior. For example, to plot the course of the Moon, astronomers could make measurements to find the Moon's position and velocity at a certain time—say, at midnight on September 1—and then use Newton's equations. Exactly what sort of measurements must be made depends on the system (it is not always position or velocity), but all systems require knowledge of their condition or state at a given time in order to plot their future course. These measurements are the *initial conditions.*

The problem is that no measurement can ever be completely accurate. There is always at least a small difference in the measured value and the true value, no matter how careful the measurement. There are always limits on precision; for instance, the length of a rope can never be measured with any greater accuracy than the smallest division of the measuring tape. This difference in the measured value and true value is called error. Unless the error is large, it is usually of little or no consequence, but there are exceptions—in chaotic systems, even a small error is a big deal.

Professor Edward N. Lorenz of the Massachusetts Institute of Technology discovered chaos in the 1960s while working with a computer program designed to predict the weather. When he provided the program with the initial conditions, it used a set of equations to calculate how the weather would evolve over time. But Lorenz noticed something peculiar. If he ran the program under one set of values for the initial conditions, then ran the program again with only slightly different values, the results were drastically different. Although the two scenarios started out at almost the same place, they quickly diverged. The only reason was the tiny change in initial conditions.

Lorenz discovered that small changes in a chaotic system that are scarcely noticeable at first can later have an enormous effect. Because of chaos, any movement or any change in the system,

Weather, such as this approaching storm, is not entirely predictable. *(Kyle Kirkland)*

no matter how small, can have dramatic consequences. This has been called the *butterfly effect*, because a butterfly flapping its wings in Texas could possibly change the course of a hurricane in the Atlantic Ocean. Perhaps this is an exaggeration, but the concept is certainly true enough, especially as far as weather systems are concerned. What this means is that if the measurement of a chaotic system's initial conditions is even slightly in error, long-range predictions will not be accurate. And since there is always some error, long-range predictions of such systems are not possible.

Mathematicians and physicists are actively studying chaos. Chaos is not a limitation of the equations of motion or a limitation of how fast or good computers are; chaos is a property of certain types of complicated systems, such as the weather. Thanks to chaos, no matter how much scientists try to understand the weather, they will never be able to make accurate predictions far in the future. Measurements can never be completely accurate, which means the knowledge of the conditions of a system will always be imperfect—and so chaos will always defeat long-range predictions for complex systems.

Rockets and Newton's Third Law

Because Newton's first and second laws of motion are so important and commonplace, people often neglect *Newton's third law*. Nature, however, remembers it quite well.

Newton's third law says that for every action there is an equal and opposite reaction. If object A exerts a force on object B, then by Newton's third law, object B exerts an equal force on A, but in the opposite direction (in terms of the force vector).

Sometimes Newton's third law can be confusing. If objects always exert equal and opposite forces on each other, how can anything ever get accelerated? Acceleration requires a force (Newton's second law), but it would seem from Newton's third law that forces always cancel each other.

But this is not what Newton's third law says—the reaction to every action does not cancel it. To analyze an object's motion, one must take into account only those forces that act on the object itself. Consider an example: a person pushes a stalled car with a certain force. Unless the car is blocked, it will begin to move, because a force (the push) acts on the car. The car is also pushing back against the person, a force that can definitely be felt in the person's hands and arms. The person pushing the car—the action—feels the reaction quite plainly. This is all that Newton's third law says. But the only forces that affect the car's motion are the forces that act on the car—in this case, the person pushing it. (There are also friction and air resistance forces acting on the car that must be included for a more complete analysis.)

Recoiling firearms are good examples of Newton's third law. The push forward given to the projectile results in a reaction, the push backward against the firearm. This is also an example of the conservation of momentum. Since the projectile and firearm initially had zero velocity and thus zero momentum, the sum of the projectile's momentum and the firearm's momentum vectors must equal zero after they start moving. Because they move in opposite directions their momentum cancels, but the much smaller mass of the bullet means that it moves much faster than the firearm so that its momentum, *mv,* equals the firearm's *mv.* Nevertheless, shooting a rifle does produce a kick. The kick can be reduced by holding the rifle tightly, because then the mass of the person combines with the rifle's mass; the much greater mass results in even less recoil velocity than with the rifle's mass alone.

The most impressive examples of Newton's third law are rockets. According to many historians, the Chinese invented rockets nearly a thousand years ago. The first use of rockets in Europe and America came in the early 19th century, such as during the War of 1812 between England and the United States. These rockets were primarily weapons and are mentioned in the national anthem of the United States: "the rockets' red glare." This refers to rockets launched from a British warship in an attack on Fort McHenry during the Battle of Baltimore, on September 13–14, 1814. These and other early rockets, however, were inaccurate and were not widely used.

Understanding the physics of rockets took a long time. Many people had the mistaken notion that rockets move by pushing against air, in the same way that people move by using their feet to push off against the ground. If this were true, rockets could only be used in the atmosphere and would be useless in the vacuum of space, where there is virtually no air. Because the physics of rockets was so poorly understood, few people worked on them or realized how useful they could be in the exploration of the solar system. Rocket science pioneers such as Robert Goddard (1882–1945) and Wernher von Braun (1912–77) corrected these misconceptions in the early and mid-20th century.

A rocket propels itself by ejecting particles with tremendous velocity in the opposite direction. This is the same way that an untied balloon full of air flies around (until the balloon exhausts its "fuel" of air). Newton's third law is at work here, as it is in recoiling firearms. A rocket engine provides an impulse equal to the product of the particles' mass, m_p, multiplied by their velocity, v_p:

$$I = m_p v_p$$

A rocket's propellant supplies both the particles and the energy needed to emit them at high velocity.

A jet engine on a plane works in a similar way to a rocket, burning fuel and ejecting gaseous molecules at high velocities. The fuel for a plane can be gasoline or some kind of combustible substance, which burns by using oxygen in the air. But often rockets must operate in space, where there is virtually no air, so rocket fuel must provide all the ingredients for its combustion. This is one of the main issues that make rocket science so difficult. In order for combustion to occur in the absence of air, rocket fuel must carry its own oxygen.

Most rockets today use chemical reactions to burn either liquid or solid propellant. A space shuttle's external tank, for example, contains a liquid hydrogen-oxygen combination with a combustion temperature of about 4,530°F (2,500°C). The particles' ejection velocity is roughly 10,000 miles per hour (16,000 km/hr).

Once physicists understood the applications of Newton's third law, rockets and jet airplanes became possible, and a huge amount of modern technology depends on these means of transportation. But nature has been using Newton's third law for a lot longer than humans have. Many marine animals employ jets for propulsion, expelling water at high velocity. The squid probably has nature's premier jet. Inside the animal is a water-filled cavity surrounded by a strong muscle; contraction of the muscle forces water through a nozzle, propelling the squid in the opposite direction. Small species of squid can reach speeds up to 20 miles per hour (32 km/hr), which is not bad for an animal that is usually not quite a foot (3.3 m) in length.

Future Spaceships

Spaceships operating today, such as a space shuttle, use chemical reactions and Newton's third law to achieve the high speeds necessary to go into orbit or escape Earth's gravity entirely. Future spaceships will probably employ similar yet possibly quite distinct means of travel—such as nuclear power or lasers—but the need for high speed will always remain. The biggest problem as far as astronauts are concerned is acceleration.

In the novel *From the Earth to the Moon* (first published in the 1860s), French writer Jules Verne wrote about a spaceship launched by a gigantic cannon. The ship was like a bullet shot into space. The idea was intriguing, but physicists who studied the details realized that it could not possibly work. Verne's hypothetical ship and its occupants would be subjected to a tremendous initial force if shot out of a cannon. According to Newton's laws of motion, this would mean they would also experience a tremendous acceleration, because $F = ma$. Such acceleration would have killed Verne's astronauts.

Inertia is the problem here. Whether an object is stopping or starting, inertia exists. When a car suddenly stops, passengers who are not wearing seat belts will keep going until they hit the dashboard or windshield. A sudden forward acceleration in a car results in passengers sliding back into their seats, as if the seat is pushing them in the back. This is inertia, because the passengers were initially at rest and would not have moved except that the car "pushed" them forward. Passengers experience this push only in times of acceleration—they do not feel motion at constant velocity (except for such things as bumps, which produce small accelerations in the vertical direction). When a car is traveling at a constant speed, so are the passengers, and there is no sensation of being pushed.

Newton's second law says that a large force produces a large acceleration—and a large push in the back for any occupants. But human beings can withstand only so much of a push. Scientists often describe accelerations in terms of Earth's gravity, because gravity is something everyone experiences. At sea level, the acceleration of an object due to gravity is 32 feet/second^2 (9.8 m/s^2); this is called one gravity or simply 1 G. Acceleration at three times this rate (96 ft/s^2, or 29.4 m/s^2) is 3 G. Astronauts riding in a space shuttle can experience accelerations of this magnitude during the early phase of their journey.

Acceleration at 3 or 4 G is not pleasant but endurable. Occupants of a ship accelerating at 4 G feel the acceleration as if it were a weight, pressing them down—the push that comes from the ship as it rapidly changes velocity—as if gravity has suddenly increased an extra four times and the astronauts "weigh" that much more. The human body is strong enough to withstand 10 times the normal body weight for a short period of time. But in Verne's novel, the astronauts would have been subjected to an acceleration of thousands of G. The poor astronauts would have been crushed into the floor with a force of many tons.

Tremendous accelerations are not compatible with human beings. To get up to high speeds, people have to take their time. A "gun" may possibly launch a ship into space but it must do so slowly. One feasible idea is to use electricity to propel a ship along a rail, like a train along a track. Unless the rail is long, it would not be able to launch the ship with sufficient speed to escape Earth's gravity, and further acceleration from more conventional engines would be needed. But the extra boost would mean less activity from the engines, which would require less fuel, and therefore less mass to accelerate—always a welcome situation in spaceship launches.

Perhaps the best way to escape Earth's gravity is to never be in it in the first place. Launching ships from space would be easy, because there is less planetary gravity to fight and no drag from the atmosphere. Since a ship would not be required to achieve a high escape velocity in a short period of time (as do ships launched from the surface of the Earth), acceleration could be gentle, slow, and human-friendly. Of course this would require ships to be built in space, perhaps hauled up from Earth in pieces and assembled

The *International Space Station* orbits Earth at an average altitude of about 225 miles (360 km). *(NASA)*

at various stations. This is entirely possible, at least in the future, and people are already starting to establish a permanent presence in space. *The International Space Station,* begun in 1998, is usually always manned by at least two or three astronauts.

One of the most exciting aspects of future spaceships is the goal to make them inexpensive enough to be affordable to many people, not just governments and corporations with huge budgets. The key is reusability. The cost per launch is high if the ship, such as a rocket, is used only once and then lost or destroyed. A ship that can be reused would greatly cut the cost per launch. This was the goal of the space shuttle when it was designed and developed in the 1970s and 1980s. Unfortunately, the space shuttle, while effective, has not reduced the expense for each launch as much as hoped. (The space shuttle is also not entirely reusable. The external fuel tank, which is necessary to hold some of the massive amount of fuel needed to achieve orbit, does not survive the launch and must be continually replaced.)

Space agencies such as NASA are currently working on ships that are entirely reusable and much more affordable. Many companies, and even some highly enthusiastic individuals, are also working on the problem. The incentives are economic as well as scientific. There are a lot of business opportunities in space, from manufacturing to tourism. But the best thing is that once people develop these ships, it will become as easy to achieve orbit as it is today to fly in an airplane across the ocean.

Safely achieving tremendous speeds to reach orbit or just traveling across Earth in less time is important for trade and the world's economy. But starting, stopping, or simply going along smoothly requires more physics than most people think. Incorporating Newton's laws of motion into the design and construction of vehicles was essential in transforming the era of slow and dangerous horseless carriages into the relatively safe, speedy era of jets and rockets that exists today. Although chaos limits the ability to deal with certain complex systems, future advances in physics will help create faster speeds and safer vehicles.

3

ROTATION

LINEAR MOTION—MOVEMENT in a straight line, involving no turning or twisting—is usually easier to understand than rotation. When objects start spinning, complications arise. But rotation is common. One of the first inventions—and still perhaps the greatest—was the wheel. The physics of rotational movement has had a tremendous impact on civilization from the very beginning.

Rotation has a profound influence on *stability*—how well an object or a system of objects is able to maintain its state. A coin placed on its edge quickly falls over, but the same coin can remain on its edge for quite a while if it is rolling, as anyone knows who has ever had to chase a dropped quarter; a rolling coin stays upright until it loses speed (unless someone steps on it, or it goes down the gutter). The same thing is basically true for bicycles and motorcycles. Once a bicycle is rolling, almost anyone can ride it, but few people can stay upright for long on a bicycle that is not moving. When a person riding a motorcycle stops for a red light, the rider maintains balance by resting a foot on the ground.

Stability is related to inertia. Objects with mass have inertia, so changing their state of motion requires a force. Making a stationary wheel start to spin also requires a force. In the absence of friction, another force is needed to stop it once it is in motion. The quantity called momentum is critical in analyzing linear motion, and a similar quantity is critical in analyzing rotational motion. This quantity is angular momentum, discussed in the sidebar on page 46.

Angular Momentum

Angular momentum, like linear momentum, is an important quantity in physics. But whereas linear momentum is mass multiplied by (linear) velocity, angular momentum is the product of something called the *moment of inertia* and ω (omega), the angular velocity. Galileo's notion of inertia applies to spinning bodies as much as to other, nonrotating bodies, and the moment of inertia is the resistance, or inertia, of a body to a change in rotational motion.

The angular velocity ω, measured in degrees of angle per second or, more often, in radians per second, is a measure of how fast an object is spinning. A rotating body turns through a certain angle, with a complete revolution comprising 360 degrees. The radian is a unit based on the radius of the rotation, with 2π radians equal to one revolution. (The Greek symbol π, or pi, represents the number 3.14159. . . .)

Angular momentum is to rotation what linear momentum is to straight, nonrotational movement. To change the linear motion of a body, one must apply a force. To change the rotation of a body, one must also apply a force. The effect of this force is called a *torque*, and it produces a change in the rotation—initiating a spin, stopping a spin, or simply changing the rate (angular velocity) or direction. Angular momentum is a vector quantity, as is linear momentum, but the angular momentum vector is differently oriented, as shown in the diagram at right. Angular momentum is a conserved quantity, as is linear momentum.

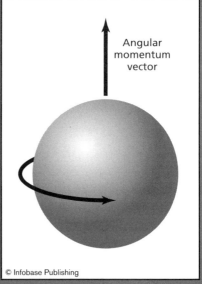

Angular momentum vector

© Infobase Publishing

For a ball rotating in the direction shown, the angular momentum vector points straight up.

Everything that spins has angular momentum, and a spinning object with a lot of mass or a high rate of spin has a great deal of angular momentum. This is what makes a rotating or rolling object stable—a large amount of force (torque, in this case) is needed to change its angular momentum, and so the object tends to continue spinning in the same fashion. Objects such as bullets, footballs, and gyroscopes are excellent examples.

Bullets, Footballs, and Gyroscopes

A gyroscope, in its simplest form, is a disk that is rotating about an axle. The axle is generally fixed on a mount, which is made in such a way that puts no force (torque) on the axle. When the gyroscope is spinning, both the disk and the axle maintain their orientation because of the conservation of angular momentum.

Gyroscopes are essential for travel in air and space. In airplanes, they provide a stable reference. An airplane can move in any direction and can find itself in any orientation—nose up or nose down, left wing up or left wing down—and sometimes it is not easy for the pilot to be sure which is the case, particularly when the airplane is moving fast and there is no visible reference marker, a situation that may occur on a dark night or in a cloud. But regardless of the orientation of the airplane, the gyroscope is stable and maintains its original position. The gyroscope's mount is attached to the airplane and so of course it changes its orientation along with the airplane, but since the mount can move without putting any torque on the axle, the gyroscope's angular momentum stays the same. The instrumentation can determine the airplane's orientation by comparing it to the gyroscope's (constant) orientation at any given instant in time. Gyroscopes are not only important for human pilots, they are critical elements for automatic pilots. The use of a gyroscope enables a sophisticated computer and an electronic control system to fly an airplane, with the gyroscope providing the necessary information on orientation.

Rotation provides stability in many other situations. A rifle bullet travels true—in a straight line to its target—because of its rotation. Rotation is so important that the rifle got its name because the barrel is rifled, meaning a spiraled groove is cut, or bored, on the inside surface. This distinguishes it from old weapons called muskets, which were usually smoothbore.

Rifling became necessary when people realized that air resistance significantly slowed down spherical bullets, such as the old musket balls. A tapered bullet, being more streamlined, was expected to travel faster and farther. The problem was that when a smoothbore gun fired such a bullet, it tumbled wildly through the air. This motion created more air resistance, making it even slower than a spherical bullet and decreasing the accuracy as well.

The solution was a lesson in physics. If a bullet is rotating very quickly, it has a lot of angular momentum and will be stable in flight. The way to give it a proper rotation is to make the bullet fit snugly in a barrel that has a spiraled groove, which sets the bullet spinning as it exits the barrel. How fast the bullet will spin is governed by how many turns the groove has and the speed of the bullet. The best spin rate depends on the bullet's size, but most rifles have grooves that turn around once per 9–12 inches (22.5–30 cm) of barrel. This may not seem like much, but bullets move quickly and exit with a high rate of spin, often thousands of revolutions per second. The groove also usually scratches a bullet in a characteristic way, and forensics experts analyze these marks in order to match bullets with the gun that fired them.

Footballs, like bullets, also spin, and for the same reason. No quarterback can throw a football with the same spin rate of a bullet, but this is not necessary. A football, being large, will be stabilized with a smaller angular velocity. Experienced quarterbacks throw tight spirals. A quarterback who fails to put enough spin on the ball throws a "wobbler" or "wounded duck" which does not fly true, and which is often intercepted and run back for a touchdown. Without the physics of rotation, the game of football would be a much different sport.

There is one thing about a football pass that confuses people (including a few physics professors). It is surprising that the nose of the football tends to track its trajectory when it is thrown in a spiral, as shown in the upper part of the diagram on page 49. In other words, the nose is pointed up when the quarterback first lofts the ball into the air, and it stays that way until it reaches the peak of the trajectory, then turns down as the ball does the same.

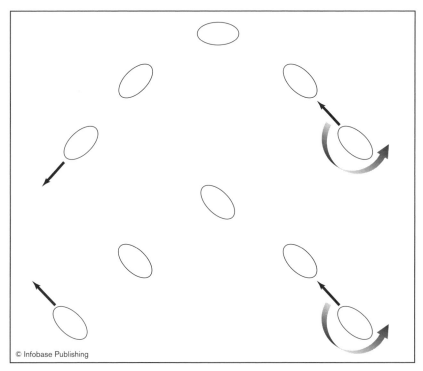

The nose of a spiraling football will usually track its trajectory, as shown in the upper illustration, because there is often a torque that alters the angular momentum. Sometimes, however, the angular momentum stays constant, as in the lower illustration.

This should not happen, because angular momentum is a vector quantity (consisting of both magnitude and direction) and should be constant during the flight, as shown in the lower part of the diagram. Sometimes footballs do behave in this manner, and the orientation stays the same throughout flight. But most of the time the angular momentum changes because of wind resistance, which produces a small but effective torque. The angular momentum in this case is not completely constant. So physics still prevails—even if the ball is intercepted and run back for a touchdown.

Coriolis Effect

Rotation affects the world in many ways. One of the most prominent effects occurs because Earth itself rotates. It was a while before people realized all the consequences of Earth's rotation, because it is not obvious to the inhabitants of Earth's surface. But when technology advanced enough to enable people to fire a projectile across a vast distance, some funny things started happening.

Armies in the Northern Hemisphere learned that if their artillery lobbed shells for long distances, the shells tended to deflect to the right. Military engineers computed ballistic tables, providing proper corrections based on distance and velocity. But during World War I the British navy learned that the opposite tendency occurred in the Southern Hemisphere. In a battle near the Falkland Islands, south of the equator, British sailors noticed their shells consistently strayed to the left. The problem was made worse because their ballistic tables assumed a rightward deflection.

The tendency of moving objects to deflect to the right in the Northern Hemisphere and to the left in the Southern Hemisphere is due to the *Coriolis effect,* named after French scientist Gaspard de Coriolis (1792–1843). The Coriolis effect occurs because Earth is a sphere and spins on its axis.

Users of artillery pieces such as this howitzer often need to consider Earth's rotation (Coriolis effect) in order to hit their target. *(U.S. Army/Spc. Aaron Ritter)*

What does the spin have to do with deflection? In any sphere that spins, including Earth, the rotational velocity of each point of the surface depends on its distance from the axis. Imagine a spinning basketball. A point near the middle (the "equator") moves quickly, while a point on the axis (say, at the finger of the player who is holding up the ball) hardly moves at all. The same situation holds true for Earth.

This difference in velocity causes a deflection in objects moving in a northern or southern direction. A rocket resting on the surface of Earth at the North Pole has no rotational velocity because it is on the axis of rotation. If the rocket is fired and heads south (which is the only direction it can go!), when it reaches, say, the latitude of Seattle, Washington (roughly 47 degrees latitude), the Earth's surface is traveling about 700 miles per hour (1,120 km/hr) around the axis, toward the east. From the rocket's perspective, the ground is moving east at 700 miles per hour (1,120 km/hr), as shown in the figure on page 52 (remember, the rocket initially had zero angular velocity because it was at the pole). From the perspective of a person standing on the ground, the rocket is moving west at 700 miles per hour (1,120 km/hr). This relative velocity, caused by the planet's rotation, means that any object moving in a northern or southern direction will drift toward the right of its path in the Northern Hemisphere. In the Southern Hemisphere, the same effect causes a deflection to the left.

The Coriolis effect is the reason that hurricanes rotate counterclockwise (as viewed from above) in the Northern Hemisphere. Storms rotate clockwise in the Southern Hemisphere. But the Coriolis effect, while strong, is only noticeable across long distances. It influences hurricanes because they can be hundreds of miles wide, but it does not strongly influence short paths or small bodies; for example, although some people claim that the Coriolis effect causes water draining from a sink to spin counterclockwise in the Northern Hemisphere, this is incorrect. Unless the sink is miles wide, the difference in rotational velocity of its parts is insignificant. The spin of water draining from a sink is due much more to the tilt of the sink or its shape.

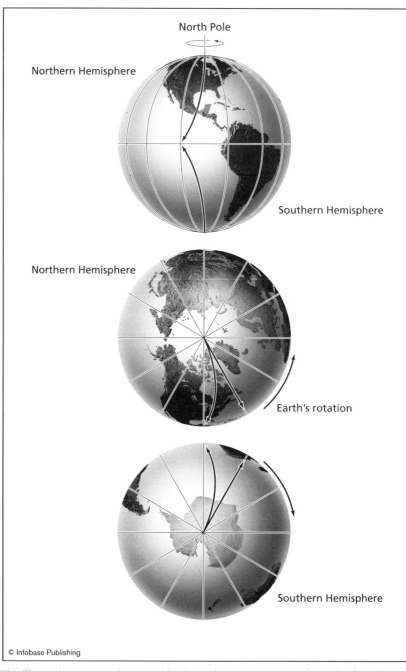

North Pole

Northern Hemisphere

Southern Hemisphere

Northern Hemisphere

Earth's rotation

Southern Hemisphere

© Infobase Publishing

The illustration on top shows a side view of the trajectories of missiles fired from the North Pole and South Pole. The bottom two illustrations show the trajectory as seen from the North Pole; the straight arrow indicates the trajectory the missile would have taken if the Earth was not rotating.

Ball Bearings

Rotation is important for both small and large objects. The rolling of a small wheel did wonders for the development of transportation. But there was a serious problem to be overcome: friction.

In every car, train, and wagon, there will always be something rubbing against something else. This is because the wheels are spinning but the car, train, or wagon is not (it is moving forward but it is not spinning). In the old days, wagons required plenty of grease; applying lubrication reduced the friction of wheels against the axle to a tolerable level.

But there is a better solution. People realized that friction could be much reduced if the two surfaces could have something placed between them—something that rolled, such as a little ball, as illustrated in the diagram below. Ball bearings started making their appearance in the 18th and 19th centuries.

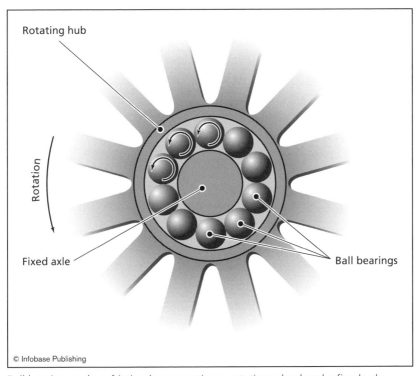

© Infobase Publishing

Ball bearings reduce friction by separating a rotating wheel and a fixed axle.

Ball bearings work because rolling is easier than sliding. Ball bearings are small spheres situated between a rotating object and one that does not rotate (or rotates at a different speed). This decreases friction because there is not as much rubbing—the ball bearings simply spin around. (Lubricant also helps here, so people do not neglect to supply it.)

Although small and mostly hidden from sight, ball bearings are extremely important in modern society. Without ball bearings, friction would waste a vast quantity of fuel. Their importance in commerce and industry was apparent during World War II, as the Allies made several costly air raids over Germany to bomb factories that produced ball bearings.

Computer Hard Disks

Rotation is important for a lot of other things that, like ball bearings, tend to be concealed. These days a huge amount of information, called data, is stored in computer hard disks, which are usually hidden inside the computer console or box. Within the computer, hard disks are rapidly spinning, which is vital for their operation. Although they cannot be seen to spin, in some computers (particularly older ones) they can usually be heard—when hard disks are in operation there is a definite whirring sound coming from the computer.

A computer's hard disk contains one or more platters that store information as magnetized bits, a "0" or a "1" in the binary, two-digit language of computers. The platters look like a set of stacked plates, with a small amount of space between each one. The space allows room for the head, which reads or writes the data. The plates are usually only a few inches in diameter and are coated with a substance such as iron oxide that can be aligned magnetically by the head.

The head reads or writes data in concentric circles called tracks. These tracks form tiny rings around the platter, and in order for the head to read and write efficiently the platters rotate at a high rate. Many computer disks spin at 3,600 to 7,200 revolutions per minute (rpm), but some of them spin at a higher rate, up to 15,000 or more rpm. This is much faster than the old phonograph music records, which rotated at 33⅓ rpm (for LP records). With such a high spin rate, reading and writing take little time, even though tremendous amounts of data are involved.

But the high spin rate creates problems. The platters must be strong in order to rotate so quickly—this is why computer hard disks are called hard—and the platters are usually made of a light but sturdy material such as aluminum. Removable disks such as floppy disks are usually light and flexible, but they cannot be rotated so quickly—typically 360 rpm. This means that it takes much more time to read and write data using floppy disks.

Artificial Gravity and Centrifuges

Sometimes people forget that rotation is an acceleration. Rotation is an acceleration even if speed is held constant, because acceleration is a change in velocity—which has two components, speed and direction. Rotation necessarily involves a continual change in direction, and any object that follows a curved path, even if only briefly, experiences rotary motion during that period of time. Motorists who make turns too quickly get reminded that rotation is acceleration because their car tires screech and slip. The tires (and the rest of the car, including the passengers) experience a force.

For angular motion, physicists speak of forces called centripetal (toward the center) and centrifugal (away from the center). Inertia plays a primary role here, as it does so often in physics. If an object in motion is left alone, it will continue moving in a straight line. The object needs a force in order to slow down or turn.

Inertia is a concern not only for speedy motorists. Computer engineers who design the hard drives mentioned earlier must consider the forces acting on the spinning platters. If a platter cannot withstand strong forces, its surface may wrinkle, ruining the disk and perhaps even causing the read-and-write head to crash.

Forces involved in rotation can also be used for productive purposes. Biological laboratories use machines called centrifuges to spin material such as cells or the components of cells. A centrifuge works by rotating a small container, usually filled with *fluid,* at an exceptionally high rate. Substances dissolved in the fluid move toward the end of the container farthest from the center of rotation, just as passengers slide in their seats away from the direction a car is turning. This happens because the speed with which substances move is based on their density. The process of centrifugation is sometimes called sedimentation; the heavier bits settle near the bottom, similar to what happens to sediments in a lake or a pond. Particles settle by gravity in a lake, but in a centrifuge the movement is due to rotational acceleration (sometimes called angular acceleration).

Centrifuges are essential to many aspects of biology and chemistry. Scientists in these fields often deal with solutions, which are mixtures of substances. Separating a mixture is frequently desirable, but sometimes this can be extremely difficult. A bag of rocks can be separated by hand, but a chemical dissolved in water cannot be removed simply by plucking out the molecules—they are too small and too many. Centrifuges help by sedimenting large molecules in solutions.

One vital substance that can be obtained through centrifugation is DNA. Forensic experts who solve crimes by examining the evidence at a crime scene will usually search for DNA, which may lead them to a suspect. But DNA is not readily removed from tissue samples found at crime scenes; most of the DNA is packed away in the nucleus of cells and can only be separated from the rest of the biological tissue by the addition of chemicals and then centrifugation.

Some centrifuges are the size of microwave ovens and even smaller, but the larger ones are the size of washing machines. Centrifuges are related, in a way, to washing machines, since both use rotation. And, as in a washing machine, it is important to maintain balance in a centrifuge, because when the load is out of balance the rotation becomes wobbly. This is even more crucial in centrifuges because some of them can spin up to 1 million rpm, producing a force millions of times greater than gravity.

The fact that rotation can produce an acceleration comparable to and even much greater than gravity suggests another use. Rotation can create what is known as artificial gravity. An important application of artificial gravity is in space, where there may not be any of the natural variety of gravity. Objects will experience weightlessness in a space habitat that is far removed from any planet, or even a habitat that is in orbit (and thus in free fall, so there appears to be no gravity, even though this is not true). People who experience weightlessness for a long period of time—months, for instance—often suffer from harmful physiological changes, which would seem to preclude long-term living in space. But these changes do not occur in a space habitat that is rotating, providing artificial gravity.

Is there any other way of producing artificial gravity? If there is, nobody has yet found it. On TV shows and movies, people walk around in apparent gravity even on nonrotating spaceships. This may be a nod to the idea that in the future, perhaps, another type of artificial gravity will be discovered. More likely, though, it's an example of artistic license on the part of the writers and producers. (Or maybe they do not know much physics.) One of the most realistic science fiction movies is *2001: A Space Odyssey*, made in 1968. The gravity produced on the ships in this movie was from rotation.

This centrifuge, located at the University of Texas Medical Branch at Galveston, allows scientists to study artificial gravity and its effects on the human body. *(NASA/JSC)*

Engineers calculate how much rotation will produce an accept-able amount of gravity by using the formula for angular accelera-tion, v^2/r, where v is the velocity and r is the radius of the rotation. This formula gives spaceship designers an idea of how fast the ship must rotate to produce a given level of acceleration that comes close to that of Earth's surface gravity of 32 feet/second^2 (9.8 m/s^2). For example, a circular or cylindrical ship a half mile (0.8 km) in diameter would need to make one revolution per minute for people at the edge (the inner surface) to feel the same pull they would on Earth.

Rotation to produce artificial gravity is a great idea, but there are problems. A diameter of half a mile (0.8 km) makes for a very large ship, and ships with a smaller, more economical radius would need to spin much faster. This would create a lot of engineer-ing problems, and life on a small rotating ship would be strange. Because of the high rotation, there would be a large Coriolis effect that would influence even small objects like kitchen sinks. It could also affect stomachs, much to the discomfort of their owners.

A Tale (Tail) of *Tyrannosaurus rex*— How a Dinosaur Maintained Balance

Tyrannosaurus rex was a species of dinosaur that lived 65–85 mil-lion years ago. It was the biggest carnivore ever to hunt on the sur-face of the Earth (although some scientists believe that members of this species were more scavengers than hunters, eating dying or dead animals rather than catching their prey). These dinosaurs could grow up to 45 feet (13.7 m) in length and could weigh nine tons (80,100 N). Their mouth held 60 teeth, each the size of a long knife—about six inches (15 cm). Fortunately for people and other relatively small mammals, *Tyrannosaurus rex* became extinct about 65 million years ago.

Scientists are not sure how fast these dinosaurs could move, and there is no agreement on exactly how they moved or just how fierce a predator they really were. From the shape of the skeleton, however, several facts are obvious. *Tyrannosaurus rex* had powerful hind legs, which were used for walking or running, but the animal

The Field Museum of Chicago, Illinois, houses this *Tyrannosaurus rex* skeleton. *(David R. Frazier/Photo Researchers, Inc.)*

had extremely small forelegs—so small as to be almost useless (how the dinosaur used them, if at all, is not known). As a result, one of the worst things that could happen to a *Tyrannosaurus rex* was to lose its balance and fall. In such an incident, unfortunately for the dinosaur (and anything that happened to be below), the animal would hit the ground hard, since the dinosaur's forelimbs were too tiny to break its fall.

A fall is basically a rotation. The feet stumble or stop, but the head and torso keep going (inertia again!), following an arc down to the ground. When humans fall, long arms help cushion the landing or prevent the person from falling all the way to the ground. People also use their arms to maintain balance, stretching them out when walking along a narrow, raised walkway such as a tightrope. (Tightrope walkers who work in a circus usually use artificially extended arms—a long pole.)

Since the arms of *Tyrannosaurus rex* were so short, if the dinosaur stumbled and fell there would be nothing to stop a crash landing of its head and torso. With a weight of nine tons (80,100 N), this would be a serious crash. Some scientists have estimated that *Tyrannosaurus rex* could reach speeds of 45 miles per hour (72 km/hr)—an example of such motion was shown in the 1993 movie *Jurassic Park*. But at that speed, and with so much mass, the animal's momentum would have been tremendous. One false step would have sent the dinosaur plunging to the ground with a fatal force.

Was *Tyrannosaurus rex* a speedy but extremely careful runner? Perhaps, but one thing scientists agree on is the purpose of the massive tail: counterbalance. With its weight evenly distributed, *Tyrannosaurus rex* had less of a chance of taking a ground-shaking spill.

Antilock Brake System

Sometimes rotary movement, such as a fall, is dangerous. But sometimes a lack of such movement is the problem.

The tires of a car grip the road, push the car forward, and change direction when the driver wants to make a turn. But tires can only do these things if they are rotating. When tires stop rotating and start to skid, the driver loses control of the car. This is very dangerous when braking, because the car will not stop—its inertia will continue to carry it forward. The driver can only stop the car by applying the brakes, which is supposed to slow and eventually stop the tire's rotation; but if the tires are skidding, the brakes do no good.

The most dangerous situations occur when the roads are slippery, such as in rain or snow. The problem is made worse because many drivers panic. When the car begins to skid, they press harder on the brake pedal. This guarantees that the car will continue to skid, because the brakes lock up the tires and keep them from rotating. Suppose a driver wishes to stop a car on a wet or icy roadway. If there is a small spot where the road surface is slippery, the tires lose traction and stop rotating—the car skids. This is not a big problem if the slippery spot is small, because the tires will begin to rotate again when the car leaves the spot and traction is regained. But if the driver slams on the brakes as the car begins to skid, this will lock up the tires—they are tightly clamped and cannot rotate, even when they reach a normal surface again, because the brakes prevent them from turning. The skid is prolonged further than necessary, and the car continues to slide out of control. This is the reason drivers used to be taught to "pump" the brakes when stopping on slippery surfaces.

But with an application of some basic physics—along with an ingenious bit of engineering—the antilock brake system (ABS) appeared. An ABS gives drivers a better chance of keeping control of their car when braking on slippery surfaces. An ABS automatically senses which tires are turning properly—and thus have traction—and will release the brake on the tires that are not turning properly (in other words, the tires that are skidding). Because brakes only work when tires are properly rotating, an ABS does not reduce braking power when it releases the brake on skidding tires. Instead, it has the benefit of preventing skidding tires from being locked up, so that when they regain traction, they can begin to rotate—at which point it is useful to apply the brake to the tire (if stopping is desired), which an ABS will do. Drivers of cars with an ABS do not need to pump the brake, and should not do so, since the system itself prevents locking.

Applications of the physics of rotation and angular momentum are widespread and include car brakes, data storage of computers, airplane instrumentation, anatomy of dinosaurs, and much else. Many objects spin, including planets. The effects are sometimes quite unusual, but with knowledge of physics, these effects can be handled with ease—and in some cases even be put to good use.

4

WORK AND ENERGY

A N UNDERSTANDING OF force and motion was instru-
mental in the development of a technological society. Among
other things it led to the ability to do work efficiently and in vast
quantity. People do not just work harder today, they work smarter,
thanks to a better knowledge of the principles of physics.

Machines that tremendously extend and supplement the work
of human beings were the result of the Industrial Revolution, which
began in Europe and America in the early 19th century. Scientists
and engineers developed steam engines, electric motors, and gigantic steel furnaces. Although machines that were marvels of the early
Industrial Revolution are now nothing but quaint antiques, the same
physics and the same ideas, in modified form, are being used today.

But machines are much older than the Industrial Revolution.
A machine is any device that helps people do work and that adds
to the sometimes meager capacity of human muscles, which are
marvelous feats of physiology but which are not quite as powerful as could be desired. Some machines are straightforward and
uncomplicated; the first machine that humans learned how to use
was probably the lever, discovered in prehistoric times.

Levers and Simple Machines

A lever is typically a kind of rigid bar that can pivot around a fixed
point, which is called the fulcrum. One of the greatest scientists in

Machines such as this crane are essential equipment in construction projects. Without this equipment, lifting steel beams or concrete blocks up to the top floors of this building under construction would require a huge number of workers, all of whom would be exposed to serious danger. *(Kyle Kirkland)*

ancient times, Archimedes (287–212 B.C.E.), supposedly said that if he were given a lever and a place to stand, he could move the world. Although he was exaggerating, he had the right idea, and today people use levers in one form or another all the time. The claw of a hammer is a lever, often used to remove embedded nails. A baseball bat is also a lever.

There are six common types of basic machines, often referred to as simple machines: lever, pulley, wheel and axle, inclined plane (ramp), wedge, and screw. These simple machines make work easier because they offer some sort of mechanical advantage. Physicists describe the manner in which machines function in terms of *work* and energy.

Work and energy, to physicists, are terms with specific meanings. Work is done when a force acts on an object and the object moves. If the force is constant, work is equal to the product of force and distance. (If the force is not constant, then an average force might be used, or if this is not feasible, the calculation must be made with a mathematical technique called integration.) If there is no force, then there can be no work done; if there is a force but it does not move an object across some distance, then there is also no work done. A person may get tired standing and holding up a heavy suitcase, but he or she has done no work, as defined in physics. The force must make an object move and the movement must be in the direction of the force in order for work to be done.

Energy is the capacity to do work. Physicists do not know how to define energy in any other way, and it is impossible to say what energy really is, in and of itself. Energy is an abstract concept, but it is useful because it helps physicists solve problems. Physicists define power as the product of energy and time, and the unit of power is the watt (or horsepower). Power is the rate at which energy is used.

Mechanical advantage does not, by itself, do work. All it does is make work easier. An excellent example is a crowbar. To pry open the lid of a crate requires an effort with or without a crowbar, but a crowbar helps because it multiplies the force a person can apply, since the bar concentrates the force on a small area. The user inserts one end of the crowbar into an opening or crack under the lid and pushes or pulls the other end. The longer the crowbar, the greater the multiplication, which is the advantage; mechanical advantage is also why people push open a door on the side opposite the hinges, as far away from these pivot points as possible. Doorknobs are generally located far from the hinges for this reason.

Mechanical advantage means that a smaller force may be applied to do the same amount of work, but there is a price to pay. The price is that this smaller force has to be applied for a greater period of time, or, in other words, over a longer distance. By using machines, people can do the same amount of work with a smaller force—and thus much less strain—if they are willing to be more patient and extend the effort over a longer period of time.

This is the idea behind a ramp. To lift a refrigerator up some steps always requires a certain amount of work, but if a ramp is used, the effort can be spread out over a distance. This may not

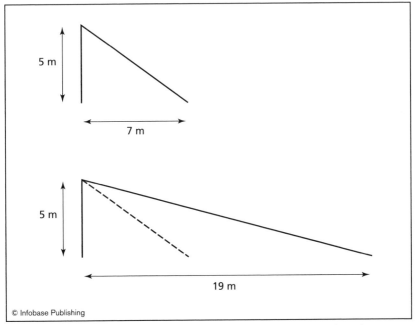

A long ramp (bottom) allows a gentler climb to the same height than does a short ramp (top; also shown as a dotted line on bottom).

only be helpful, it may be necessary, since the refrigerator may be so heavy that the movers cannot pick it up. The more gentle the incline, the less the force that is required—but the longer the ramp will have to be, which means the longer this smaller force will have to be applied, as shown in the diagram. Working on the same principle is the screw, which is essentially a ramp wound around a cylinder.

People have been using simple machines for a long time. Hunters in ancient societies often employed a stick called an atlatl, in which a notched end could hold a spear. The atlatl enabled them to throw a spear farther because it gave them leverage.

But simple machines are not always so simply applied. Engineers and scientists in the ancient world produced some amazing structures. The Great Pyramid of Khufu (also known as Cheops), built near Cairo, Egypt, about 4,500 years ago, is a staggering example. The original height was 480 feet (146 m), and the structure consists of more than 2 million blocks of stone, with an average weight of about 2.5 tons (22,250 N). Some of the materials, such as gigantic granite blocks, were hauled from quarries located 620 miles (1,000 km) away. Another great engineering accomplishment of the ancient world is the Stonehenge monument, located in England. Built between 4,000 and 5,000 years ago, it is composed of massive stones as heavy as 40 tons (356,000 N), some of which were hauled for 20 miles (32 km) or more. Historians are not certain exactly how people in ancient civilizations performed these spectacular feats of engineering, or how many laborers were required, but it is clear that these ancient engineers were well schooled in the use of machines.

The Unlikelihood of Perpetual Motion

Wonderful phenomena have been attempted throughout history, in ancient times as well as today. One of the most common things people have tried to make is known as a perpetual motion machine.

Machines capable of perpetual motion would run forever. Unlike the machines people use every day, which require energy to do work, some of these machines seem to offer the hope of doing work for free—if they exist. A large number of inventors have made such claims over the years and have filed patents at the U.S. Patent Office in order to profit from their inventions. The unfortunate reality is that none of these machines function.

Perpetual motion machines, as conceived in these unsuccessful attempts, do not mean the same things as, say, an orbiting satellite. The satellite is perpetually in motion and does not need any pushing or pulling—it is in free fall. But a satellite's motion could not be used to do work. Or, rather, it could, if some way could be devised to harness its motion and turn it into electricity, for instance. But the problem is that the satellite would not remain in orbit very long if this were done, because the velocity of the satellite would decrease and, eventually, it would fall to the ground. The energy to do work has to come from somewhere, and in satellites that somewhere would have to be either their *kinetic energy* or the *potential energy* due to their height. In either case, take away the energy and the satellite drops.

Yet there have been many claims of machines that are able to produce energy out of nothing. These machines supposedly can do enormous amounts of work but require little or no input—they would be able to generate endless amounts of energy. But it is a common experience that a machine with no input of energy will eventually stop. Cars need gasoline, or they will not run. After a while, batteries die. Solar-powered cells require sunshine, or they do not operate. Even people need fuel and must eat to live. There seems to be no such thing as a free ride in this world.

Physicists developed the scientific concept of energy in the 19th century, and with careful measurements they determined that energy is a conserved quantity. As discussed in the following sidebar, energy can be transformed into one type or another, but it cannot be created or destroyed.

There are many types of energy: electrical, nuclear, kinetic, chemical, gravitational, and thermal (heat) are examples. Energy is the capacity to do work, and work will not get done without it. In the process, energy of one type may be converted into another, but it still exists and in the same quantity as before. This has extremely

Conservation of Energy

In his textbook *Lectures on Physics*, Richard Feynman (1918–88), an American physicist who received a share of the 1965 Nobel Prize in physics, described *conservation of energy* in this simple way: "It says that there is a numerical quantity which does not change when something happens." That quantity is energy.

This is only useful if formulas are available to calculate energy. Since energy has many different forms, there are many different formulas. For example, the formula for kinetic energy (the energy due to an object's motion) is $1/2mv^2$, where m is the object's mass and v is the velocity. Physicists use the formulas to calculate the energy before and after something happens—a collision or an explosion or someone slipping and falling on an icy sidewalk. No matter what happens, the total energy before and after is always the same. Energy is conserved.

Sometimes people say that engines or generators produce energy—giving the impression that the engine somehow created the energy out of nothing—and that processes such as lifting a weight consume energy. These statements actually refer to a transformation of energy. Potential energy is a stored form of energy that can be transformed into work and kinetic energy. For example, gasoline contains a considerable amount of potential energy. In the operation of a car, the engine transforms this potential energy into the movement of the car and, although undesired, also into heat that raises the temperature of the engine and subsequently that of the hood and the surrounding frame of the car. Heat in this case is wasted energy, since this part of the gasoline's potential energy fails to get converted into motion.

important consequences, and some things are highly unlikely: *free energy machines*, for example.

To many people, the concept that energy cannot be created is quite disappointing. An understanding of physics should allow people to do great things, such as building the Great Pyramid of Khufu (which was the tallest structure in the world for more than 4,000 years). Physics should give engineers and scientists more and higher abilities, not take them away; it should fulfill dreams, not crush them. But disappointing as it is, the conservation of energy appears to be an unavoidable truth. And it is a worthwhile finding, for it prevents people with an understanding of physics from wasting their time on unlikely or even impossible pursuits.

The law of energy conservation does not, however, prevent people from searching for violations of this law. The claims of free energy inventors probably will continue. One of the most famous claims of all time was made in the late 19th century by entrepreneur John Worrel Keely. He demonstrated on several occasions a motor that seemed to be able to run on virtually nothing, and he even claimed his motor could drive a ship to England and back using only a gallon (3.8 L) of water. (At the time, people paid a lot of money to cross the Atlantic in expensive steamships.) Based on the impressive demonstrations, which were conducted at Keely's house, many people believed him and invested millions of dollars in Keely's company. But no useful device was ever developed. After Keely's death, investigators searched his house and found hidden pipes and sources of compressed air. Keely's motor was a fraud, driven by concealed energy inputs.

Many other claims have been based not on fraud but on measurement errors. The goal of free energy machines is to produce a machine that puts out more energy than it takes in—this would create energy out of nothing. But no machine has ever been able to do this, because when all sources of energy inputs are accounted for by careful measurements, the conservation of energy is always upheld. It is the undefeated champion of the world.

The laws of physics may not always let people do what they want, but physics does provide enormously useful rules. Perhaps one day someone will find an exception to the conservation of energy, but at the present time this appears doubtful.

Work and Energy of the Human Body

The laws of physics do not hold just for machines and mechanical objects, they also apply to people. Human beings are remarkably efficient and durable. Engineers have been trying for years to build robots or other machines that can perform as well as people on tasks involving agility and perception, but so far most efforts have fallen short. Various technologies can give machines superior performance in certain tasks—a combustion engine can propel a car to much faster speeds than a person can run, and computers can do arithmetic much quicker—but humans excel at many tasks involving intelligence or nimble manipulation of objects.

Human limbs behave as levers, and muscles are the engines that drive them. Muscles do work the same way as other objects: as a force acting over a distance. In the case of muscles, however, this force always comes from contraction—muscles do work by pulling. They can only apply a force as they get shorter, or as they contract, in other words. Because of their structure, muscles cannot push, which means that they cannot exert a force while extending (getting longer). A muscle can lengthen, of course, but only passively—something must be stretching it.

Because muscles can only pull, they generally work in pairs. A person raises a forearm by contracting the biceps, a strong muscle in the front part of the upper arm. The biceps gets shorter, pulling up the forearm, which rotates at the elbow joint. But the biceps cannot push the forearm down; the arm must either fall by gravity, or if force is to be applied on the downward swing (such as to hammer a nail), the triceps muscle, located at the back of the upper arm, is needed. When the triceps muscle contracts, the forearm rotates downward.

Muscles are attached to the bones by tendons. A muscle contracts, pulling on the bone. The skeleton is essential for motion, for without something hard to act on, contracting muscles would not do much good. In many animals without an internal skeleton, such as insects, the outside part of the body acts like an external skeleton, providing levers for muscles to pull.

Human muscles move limbs as levers, but the human body is not able to produce a lot of force. Human muscles are generally not attached to give powerful leverage; instead, they are efficient at applying a small force over a long period. Humans are better at slow, steady work rather than at terrifically fast, powerful effort. This is different, for example, from the jaw muscles of a crocodile

Alligators such as this one, photographed near NASA's Kennedy Space Center in Florida, have jaw muscles that can apply a tremendous amount of force. *(NASA)*

or an alligator, which apply a large force over a small distance, giving these animals such a fearsome bite.

Locomotion is one of the most important jobs for human bones and muscles. Sometimes people walk, sometimes they run. There is a definite distinction between the two, and the principles of physics are the reason people run at high speed and walk at low speed.

When people walk, at least one foot is on the ground for much of the time, and the knee of the leg supporting most of the weight is nearly straight. But during running, both feet are off the ground at times, and the knees are bent. Most people use the walking motion for speeds less than about 6.6 to 7.5 feet/second (2.0–2.3 m/s), or about five miles per hour (8 km/hr), and the running motion for higher speeds. People do this automatically, without even thinking about it. This makes a lot of sense to a physicist, because walking at a slow speed is more efficient than running—it wastes less energy. Conversely, at high speed, running is more efficient than walking. Humans are by their very nature economical when it comes to energy.

Humans are efficient walkers and runners. But sometimes people enjoy burning a little excess energy and staying in good shape, like these walkers and joggers in Fairmount Park in Philadelphia, Pennsylvania. *(Kyle Kirkland)*

Although humans are efficient, agile, and intelligent, human muscles are not able to generate much power. People are capable of averaging only about 100 watts over a long period of time (though about 1,500 watts can be generated for a brief period). Cattle can do better and are capable of sustaining 300 watts. Compare that to the many thousands or even millions of watts available from energy sources such as gasoline or electricity. But the best energy bargain of all is the human brain. It uses only about 4 watts of power and yet produces a fantastic amount of art, literature, and science.

Bicycles and Gears

Energy is scarce, but today's society involves a lot of travel and transportation, which requires work. It is vital that this is done efficiently, like the economical way that people transition from a walking style to a running style at the speed for which this transition saves effort and wastes less energy (for instance, by producing unnecessary heat). To do otherwise is to squander resources.

But the most efficient means of human locomotion is not walking or running. Riding a bicycle is probably the best way to go.

Bicycles are not only useful for moving on land, they are also effective, with appropriate modification, for moving in air. In 1979, a bicyclist named Bryan Allen flew a 75-pound (334-N) airplane, the *Gossamer Albatross,* more than 20 miles (32 km) across the English Channel. The flight lasted nearly three hours and was powered by Allen's pedaling, which turned the plane's propeller. Paul MacCready, a physicist and engineer, designed the craft.

The type of bicycle people ride today was first invented in the 1880s. Considering the efficiency and widespread application of bicycles, it is surprising that enterprising inventors did not bring about these machines earlier. However, the first bicycles—developed in the 1860s—were awkward. Perhaps it was difficult at the time to see their true value.

Strangely enough, concern over efficiency was responsible for the poor design of the early bicycles. The pedals were directly attached to the front wheel; for one revolution of the pedals, the front wheel would also make one revolution. To make this efficient, the front wheel needed a large diameter, for this size maximized the distance the wheel will turn. If the wheel were small, it would not travel very far with one revolution, and so the pedals must be turned often. But since the wheel was large, the circumference was large and one revolution covered a considerable distance. This was a way of giving the rider the most distance per revolution of the pedal. The problem was that the huge size of the front wheel required long legs to reach the pedals. The rear wheel had to be little, otherwise the rider would have had to be a giant in order to ride the bike. The figure on page 74 shows what these early bicycles looked like.

The development of chain drives vastly improved the situation. Instead of pedals being attached directly to a wheel, the rotary motion of the pedals turned the wheels via a chain and a series of basic but important machines called gears.

Gears transfer rotational motion from one place to another. In general, gears are toothed wheels that come in many different shapes and sizes, and they are found everywhere—gears drive the

The large front wheel of this old-fashioned bicycle means that the rider does not have to pedal very quickly.

hands of a clock, and huge gears turn the propeller of a cruise ship.

Gear teeth mesh together, ensuring the transfer of motion. Gears always work in pairs, one to do the driving (in other words, to transmit the rotation) and the other to be driven. This gives rise to the notion of a gear ratio, which is the ratio between the size of the driving gear and the size of the driven gear. In low gear, a relatively small gear drives a large one, and vice versa for a high gear. Each revolution of the pedal of a bicycle, for example, turns the rear wheel an amount that is governed by the chosen gear. In a high gear, pedaling turns the wheel with a greater speed, which is excellent for cruising. In a low gear, pedaling does not make the wheel turn as quickly but it provides a greater force, making low gears useful for climbing hills. Some bicycles have as many as 21 gears, though ten-speed bicycles (having 10 gears) are more common. The figure illustrates low and high gear for a ten-speed bicycle.

Automobiles also have gears. Combustion of fuel in a car's engine drives the up-and-down motion of pistons, which rotates the crankshaft. A gearbox links the motion to the axle. The driver changes the gears in cars with manual transmissions, but a machine does the job in cars with automatic transmissions. The transmission of a car is a compartment with gears connecting two shafts: one shaft, the input, carries power from the engine, and the other shaft, the output, connects with the axle, which can be either the front or rear axle, which turns the wheels. (The rear axle receives the power in rear-wheel-drive cars, and the front axle does so in front-wheel-drive cars. In four-wheel-drive vehicles, both front and rear axles may receive the power.) When the driver or the machine selects a transmission gear, a specific combination

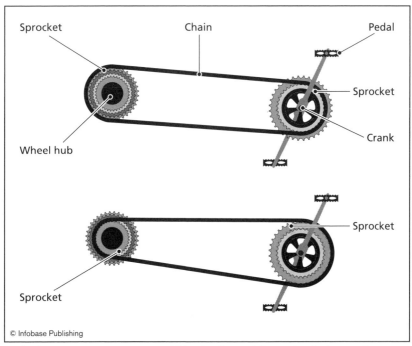

In the lowest gear on a ten-speed bicycle, the pedal sprocket is the smallest one and the wheel sprocket, which drives the wheel, is the largest (top). The opposite is true in highest gear (bottom).

of gears transmits the power from the engine to the axle or axles. The chosen gear ratio determines the transformation of engine speed to axle speed (and thus wheel speed). The most efficient gear for a given situation can be chosen by the driver or, with automatic transmissions, the machine.

Disengaging the gears (neutral gear) allows the engine of a car to run without moving the wheels at all. This is quite useful, since otherwise idling would not be possible, making it necessary to turn off the engine at every stop. And without any gears at all, starting a car would be an interesting and perilous event. A direct linkage between engine and axle would mean the wheels would always have to turn at the engine speed. The moment the engine turned on, the wheels would start spinning at the same rate—jackrabbit starts and spinouts would be unavoidable!

The Potential in Potential Energy

Bicycles are excellent machines that allow people to travel efficiently, but riding a bicycle still requires energy. Finding energy sources would not seem to be a big problem, though—energy exists everywhere. Almost everything has the capacity to do work, at least a little. But all this potential energy must somehow be extracted—converted into the kinetic energy that drives today's technological society.

Potential energy is energy that is stored and waiting to be used, and it exists in many forms. Lifting a heavy weight results in potential energy, because the weight can do work when it falls. Many countries, for example, use falling water to drive huge turbines housed in dams, such as the Hoover Dam on the Arizona-Nevada border in the United States.

Energy sources include gravitational potential energy, chemical potential energy (existing in substances such as gasoline), nuclear potential energy, electrical potential energy, and others. People use these resources for many things, including automobiles, TV sets, lights, toasters, and submarines.

Efficient conversion of potential to kinetic energy requires an understanding of physics and a lot of engineering skill. But there are other factors that must be considered, which unfortunately have been neglected until recently. There are two major disadvantages to the sources of energy that society most often relies on today: pollution and depletion. These energy sources pollute air and water, and they are not renewable. If they continue to be used at the current rate, they will soon be gone.

About 75 percent of the energy in use today comes from coal, oil, and gas. These excellent sources of energy are burned for their chemical potential energy. But the combustion process also produces pollution, such as the smog that envelopes many large cities. In principle, much of the pollution can be avoided, and chemists, physicists, and engineers have tried to make the fuel combustion process as clean as possible. But doing this is expensive, which would make these sources of energy much less affordable.

Adding to the burden is the increasing use of energy in the world today. Consumption is rising about 2 percent annually. Although that does not sound like much, it adds up. Twenty years ago, energy needs were only about two-thirds what they are today. This kind of growth is not supportable. Oil and gas reserves may last another 100 years, and coal may still be available for several centuries, but eventually they will run out. There is currently no way of producing them except by depleting what already exists— which took nature millions of years to produce.

Most people do not realize the extent of the problem. Many people see electricity as clean and cheap, but this attitude demonstrates a poor understanding of the physics of work and energy. Electricity must be generated by some process or other and thanks to the laws of physics, there is no such thing as a free ride. The burning of coal or oil generates a large portion of electricity in the United States. Even though plugging in an appliance may seem completely harmless to the environment, the process of making the electricity that runs the appliance creates pollution and uses up scarce, limited resources.

But energy is conserved! Energy is never created or destroyed, merely transformed into one type or another, so why is there a problem? The problem is that there is another law of physics, the second law of thermodynamics, that says at least some energy in every process is always converted to a form that is extremely difficult or impossible to use. The energy still exists, but nobody can get much if any work out of it. This is why a perpetual motion machine is unlikely, even if it produced no free energy at all. In all processes, regardless of what they are, some energy will "leak" away and is "lost" (that is, converted into this hard-to-use form). The more efficient a machine is, the smaller the loss of energy, but it is not possible to make it zero. What this means is that not only is it impossible to produce a machine that produces a profit in terms of energy (in the form of extra or free energy)—it is impossible to produce a machine that simply breaks even. Everything has a cost.

One of the biggest challenges of physics today is to develop alternative sources of energy. There is much potential energy in sunlight, wind, sea waves, chemical processes involving abundant substances such as hydrogen, and much else. Machines allow people to do vast amounts of work efficiently and safely, but all machines need energy. Perpetual motion machines and free energy are almost certainly not achievable, but there is no law of physics that prevents any number of potential energy sources to be tapped cleanly and, just as importantly, without danger of using them up any time soon.

5

ELASTICITY

EVERYONE PREPARES FOR the future by storing things that will be needed later. People keep food in a refrigerator or freezer, football coaches often wait until the end of a close game to call the best play, and conservationists preserve the environment so that it will continue to be used and enjoyed by generations to come.

Storing energy is also a good idea. Batteries are a common way of storing electrical energy, providing power to shine a flashlight or crank an automobile engine, and there are many other forms of potential energy, as described in the previous chapter. One way of storing mechanical energy is by bending or deforming something that has *elasticity*. Because of elasticity, the object will regain its shape once it is released, and when this happens the object can do work. Catapults and an archer's bow are good examples of this idea; the user stretches or bends a slender pole or string, which when released will rebound—and anything resting on it goes flying away at a great speed.

Not every substance has much elasticity. Materials that are stretchable or deformable but will "remember" their original shape are best. People use elastic materials in a lot of ways, and even though these materials seem simple and old-fashioned, without elasticity much of the equipment found in almost every home or neighborhood would not work.

Trampolines and Rubber Bands

The atoms and molecules that compose an object provide its elasticity. Bonds between the atoms and molecules get pulled apart as the object becomes deformed, and in some materials these bonds snap back with considerable force. Trampolines and rubber bands are made of such materials. A jumping person stretches the trampoline bed when he or she lands, stretching the bonds holding together the trampoline's molecules. When these molecules rebound, they provide enough force to send the person sailing into the air again.

Some materials, on the other hand, show little elasticity. When these materials are stretched or compressed, they do not bounce back with much force. But all materials have at least some elasticity, including wood, which is not a bouncy material but has a little elasticity. Even a small amount of elasticity can be critical; wood's elasticity is essential for carpenters—otherwise nails would not hold wooden boards together. A nail deforms the wood by pushing it aside, and the wood pushes back as it tries to regain its shape. This is the force that holds the nail in place.

Elasticity also generates the bounce when something falls to the ground. If a rubbery *superball* drops to a hard floor, it will bounce almost to the height from which it fell. (The ball can go even higher, but only if it was thrown downward—in other words, if it was given an initial velocity instead of being dropped.) An object made of wood bounces, though not much. A beanbag falls to the floor and stays there with hardly a single bounce at all. Bounciness is an important property of objects, and physicists measure it by using the *coefficient of restitution,* as discussed in the sidebar on page 81.

Sometimes bouncing is not desirable, in which case a small coefficient of restitution is needed. When objects collide, elasticity causes them to bounce apart quickly. But engineers design automobiles to prevent this from happening by equipping the frame of the car with crumple zones to absorb the energy of impact. The front and back of the car crumple and deform in an accident inelastically—the materials have little tendency spring back into

Coefficient of Restitution

Suppose an object such as a tennis ball slams into a brick wall. The tennis ball rebounds at a certain speed, and different balls will have different rebound speeds even if they collide with the wall at the same velocity; an old, tattered tennis ball does not rebound as strongly as a new, fresh one. The coefficient of restitution is a measure of elasticity because it is a ratio of the rebound speed to the initial speed of the object.

The value of the coefficient of restitution is always less than one—conservation of energy says that the ball cannot gain speed in a collision unless it hits something that is moving. (For instance, if the ball collides with a car moving in the opposite direction, the ball can rebound with a faster speed than it had initially, since the moving car pushes it.) To measure the coefficient of restitution accurately means using a flat, immobile wall or obstacle, so that the object's elasticity is measured instead of the momentum it picks up from the collision. The coefficient of restitution for most objects does not depend much on the initial speed, and so the objects lose about the same fraction of the initial speed whether they are moving quickly or slowly. This means that the coefficient is an accurate, general measure of elasticity.

Elastic objects rebound with a higher speed than do relatively inelastic objects, so they have a higher coefficient of restitution. A fresh tennis ball is more elastic than an old one. A superball may have a coefficient of restitution as high as 0.9, which means it rebounds with 90 percent of its original speed. Since kinetic energy is proportional to the square of the speed, the superball retains 0.9^2 (0.81) of its kinetic energy—81 percent. (The collision transforms the "lost" energy into heat and work.) As discussed below, tennis balls used in professional tournaments have a carefully regulated coefficient of restitution. A beanbag has a coefficient somewhere around 0.05, meaning this relatively inelastic object hardly rebounds at all.

their former shape. If the impact between two cars was elastic they would jump apart, and passengers would suffer severe and probably injurious acceleration during the bounce. The energy of the collision is not stored—the energy is not needed or wanted—and instead gets turned into heat and work that permanently changes

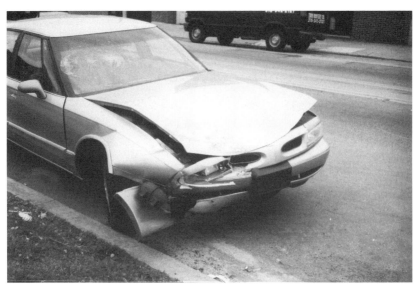

The body of the car absorbs some of the energy of impact by crumpling. *(Kyle Kirkland)*

the car (at least until the owner takes it to a body shop). An inelastic collision means that the cars are damaged but the people tend to be safe.

In other situations bouncing is the whole purpose—jumping on trampolines, for instance. Flexible nets and mats have been around a long time, and in ancient times people used to jump on blankets or skins that were stretched and held by stakes or by other people. The modern trampoline appeared in the 1930s, and the name comes from *trampolín,* the Spanish term for diving board. Trampoline beds consist of nylon or a similar material with a lot of elasticity. The thickness of the bed is only a fraction of an inch—a few millimeters—but it is strong; when a person lands on the material it stretches, and then rebounds, sending the person aloft again.

During World War II, the United States Navy used trampolines in pilot training programs. The exercise was part of the physical conditioning routine and gave the pilot trainees some practice in aerial awareness. Astronauts have also trained with trampolines. Although the descent phase of the jump only lasts a few seconds, it mimics the "weightless" conditions encountered in space.

One of the inventors of the trampoline, George Nissen, suggested the device was good for play and sports as well as for training. Nissen once managed to bring a kangaroo along with him as he jumped up and down on a trampoline. A kangaroo, well known for its hopping ability, has a natural talent for the sport.

But some people have criticized the trampoline for being hazardous. Young children are particularly prone to injuries, such as falling onto the ground, falling in the space between the trampoline bed and the frame, and landing awkwardly on the bed itself. Yet with proper training and supervision the trampoline can be a lot of fun and trampolining is a worthwhile sport. Beginning in 2000, trampolining even became part of the Olympic Games.

Rubber is another substance that is well known for its elasticity. Rubber balls have a high coefficient of restitution, and rubber bands make excellent flexible binders. (When stretched across a finger and released, they also make missiles that are dangerous to unprotected eyes.)

Natural rubber is made from the sap of trees such as *Hevea brasiliensis* and *Ficus elasticus*. This material has a great deal of elasticity, but its usefulness is limited because it tends to lose elasticity fairly rapidly, especially in extreme temperatures. Not until the 1840s, when Charles Goodyear invented a process called vulcanization, could rubber find many applications; in vulcanized rubber, the molecules become cross-linked together, retaining their elasticity for much longer and under a wider range of temperatures. Rubber fills a huge number of jobs as tires, rubber bands, erasers (one of rubber's earliest applications and the one that provided its name) and can be found everywhere in the world. It can even be found in places well beyond this world: some of the Apollo astronauts who went to the Moon used rubber bands to keep their gear and other objects from floating away.

Tennis Balls and Rackets

Tennis is another sport that involves elasticity. In tennis, the two major pieces of equipment—balls and rackets—store energy because of their elastic properties.

Tennis balls are made of two pieces of rubber sealed together, with a coating of wool or synthetic fiber on top. Inside the ball is air under high pressure, and most of the bounce of a tennis ball comes from this compressed air. After a while the air escapes, so the ball becomes flat and unusable.

The balls used in professional tennis tournaments must conform to a rigorous set of characteristics. For example, they must have just the right amount of bounce—no more and no less. The regulations specify that a ball must bounce from 53 to 58 inches (134.5 to 147.2 cm) when dropped from a 100-inch (253.8-cm) height onto a hard, flat surface. This means they have a coefficient of restitution of 0.728 to 0.762, and tennis ball manufacturers test their products to ensure the balls meet these specifications. The reason for this strict regulation is that players can judge a ball's behavior much better as it rebounds from the court surface if the coefficient of restitution for all the balls is about the same. It would be interesting to watch if someone slipped a superball with a coefficient of restitution of 0.9 into a tournament.

Tennis players are also choosy about their rackets. Years ago, all rackets were made of a wood frame and stringed with fibers from "gut"—the intestines of animals (mostly sheep and cattle). These days there are many more choices, and rackets have gotten bigger because the strength of the frame has increased and can now support a larger area.

A racket consists of strings instead of solid material because of air resistance. A stringed racket encounters a lot less air resistance than does a racket with a solid surface, so players can swing faster and harder with a stringed racket. But in order to function correctly, the strings must have the right combination of strength, elasticity, and durability. The frame of the racket holds and stretches the strings, and the elasticity is essential because the player does not want the ball to lose much energy after colliding with the racket. In an inelastic collision, the ball's velocity as it leaves the racket would be solely due to the player's swing; with an elastic collision some of the rebound speed is due to the bounce.

The tightness of the strings on a tennis racket is an important factor. Most professional tennis players tell beginners that loose strings give more power to their swing, whereas tight strings give more control. This rule, although something of an oversimplification, is true to a certain extent. Loose strings act like a trampoline, stretching when the ball collides and then snapping back, giving the ball an extra boost. Strings that are under a lot of tension act more as a rigid surface, from which the ball will bounce quickly and controllably though not with as much rebound energy. Professional players vary widely in their preferences of how much tension to use.

String composition is also critical, and string material comes in a number of different types. Many modern rackets are made with synthetic fibers instead of gut. Gut strings are expensive today but are still used by some players, particularly professionals, because these strings have an excellent combination of toughness and elasticity.

Springs

Stretch a spring and let it go. After some bouncing, the spring returns to its initial position, which is a point of equilibrium, since this is its natural length when the spring is not under any force. Like superballs and tennis balls, springs are highly elastic.

Springs are often coils of metal wire, although they can have a variety of different shapes and sizes. When a spring is compressed or stretched, it pushes or pulls on whatever is preventing it from returning to its equilibrium length, as illustrated in the figure on page 86. This force, F_r, is called a restoring force. A simple equation called *Hooke's law* quantifies this force:

$$F_r = kx,$$

where x is the distance the spring has been compressed or stretched and k is a constant. The value of k is a characteristic of a particular spring and is a measure of stiffness. The higher the value of k, the greater the restoring force of the spring.

Hooke's law, named after British physicist Robert Hooke (1635–1703), describes the behavior of many objects, not just springs, so the law is applicable in many situations involving elasticity. For

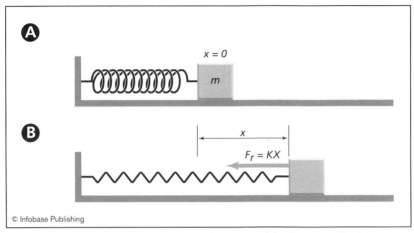

(A) The spring is in its resting (equilibrium) position. (B) When stretched or compressed, a spring's restoring force, F_r, is the product of x, the distance it has moved, and k, a constant whose value depends on the stiffness of the spring.

most elastic objects, the force exerted in the process of restoring shape is proportional to the distance it has been deformed or distorted. The only factor that changes is k, which differs for a given material.

Springs are simple devices, yet they continue to play a lot of important roles in today's society. Like many simple devices, such as gears and levers, springs are often hidden from view. Motorists ride on springs every time they drive a car, because the suspension system of most cars uses springs. These springs vary in shape—some are coiled and some are not—but they are typically quite stiff (they have large spring constants) since they must bear heavy loads and endure strong forces. Driving 3,000 pounds (13,350 N) of metal and plastic down a hard and bumpy asphalt surface at 60 miles per hour (96 km/hr) would be unbearable without them. The horse-driven coaches of the past did not go as fast but lacked adequate suspension systems, and as a result they sometimes arrived at their destination with at least one passenger suffering a broken limb, and the rest of the passengers decorated with a substantial number of black-and-blue marks.

One of the important jobs of a spring in a car's suspension is to keep all four wheels on the ground, even if the road surface is uneven. Bumps and potholes compress or stretch the springs rather than causing the rigid frame of the car to move up and down. But springs tend to bounce, even if they are stiff, and bouncing would not make a smooth, comfortable ride. It is the job of another component of the suspension system, the shock absorber, to dampen the bounce or vibration of the springs.

Many people also sleep on springs, and for basically the same reason that they ride on them. Like the springs in a car, mattress springs give way whenever required but maintain a firm support, and return to their natural length afterward—at least until their elasticity breaks down and the molecules of the material no longer snap back into place. Although Hooke's law is general and applies to a lot of situations, it has its limits. Stretch a spring too far and it breaks—no more restoring force. Springs do not last forever, and mattresses need to be replaced after a number of years because the springs wear out.

Humans have made many uses of elastic material, but, as usual, so does nature. Perhaps the most interesting function that elasticity performs is in the spine of a cheetah. The cheetah is the world's fastest animal and can run for short distances at speeds up to 70 miles per hour (112 km/hr). The biology of these animals

The energy stored and released in the cheetah's spine helps this animal to achieve speeds up to 70 miles per hour (112 km/hr). *(G. Ronald Austing/Photo Researchers, Inc.)*

is strongly adapted for its speedy lifestyle, and they use elasticity to great effect. The backbone of a cheetah is highly elastic, so when compressed the spine "uncoils," providing a surge of force to propel the cheetah as the animal leaps forward. The cheetah then lands on its front feet, and the back end of the animal keeps moving forward, compressing the spine. When the animal plants the back feet and lifts the front feet again, the spine releases its energy for the next leap. The cheetah's spine is like a horizontal pogo stick that helps the animal achieve its astonishing speed.

The uses of elasticity in the world are many and varied, from springs in mattresses and rubber in tennis balls to the elastic spines of cheetahs. Elastic objects rebound, and when they do, much of the energy used to compress or stretch them gets returned. These materials pay back the user, though not in full—the coefficient of restitution is generally less than 1.0—but at least in part. A cheetah's backbone is one of nature's best examples of elasticity, the same property that helps a tennis racket send a ball flying away with great speed. When the bonds holding a material together can snap the molecules back into their original configuration after being bent or compressed, the resulting force can be substantial.

6

OSCILLATIONS

ONE OF THE best-known symbols of freedom in the United States is the Liberty Bell; made in the 1750s and located in Philadelphia, Pennsylvania, its ringing has marked important events throughout history. Because of the crack, which occurred sometime in the middle of the 19th century, people no longer ring the Liberty Bell, but they softly tap it every Fourth of July to commemorate Independence Day.

All bells ring—that is their purpose—but ringing is a common phenomenon. All objects "ring" to some extent, and a back-and-forth movement—a wave or *oscillation*—occurs frequently in nature. Everything that people hear comes from waves in the air, set in motion by some disturbance or movement. This movement causes air molecules to speed away and collide with each other, generating areas of high and low pressure called sound waves. Speech and music belong in this category. Waves can also be violent, such as earthquakes, which are waves that travel through rocks and soil. But waves can yield a lot of information, and geologists study earthquakes to get a better understanding of the interior of the planet. Physicians also use waves to see inside the human body. This chapter discusses waves and some of the many ways they affect people and the world in which they live.

To understand waves, a person need only get the rhythm. Everything has one.

Frequency and Wavelength

A wave, or oscillation, is a motion that repeats, such as a wave traveling down a taut string, as diagrammed in the figure. All waves or oscillations possess certain simple characteristics. A given point on the string vibrates about its resting (equilibrium) position, and the greatest distance it moves—the crest—is called the wave's *amplitude*. The *wavelength* is the distance between two crests of the wave. The frequency of the wave is the number of crests that pass a given point in one second; this is the same as the number of cycles of the wave that occur in one second.

Frequency and wavelength are related to one another: A high-frequency wave has a short wavelength, and a low-frequency wave has a long one. This can be seen from the follow-

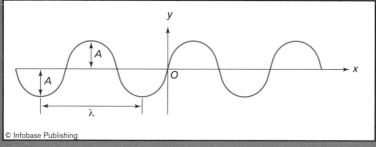

© Infobase Publishing

Important properties of a wave include its amplitude, A, and its wavelength, λ.

Getting the Rhythm: Natural Frequencies and Resonance

Ringing is a periodic motion. Such vibrations are called oscillations— a repetitive cycle of motion, moving back and forth. Oscillations have a *frequency*, which is the number of cycles per second (*cps*). For example, if an oscillation goes back and forth three times in a second, it has a frequency of 3 cps. Another name for cps is *Hertz*, named in honor of Heinrich Hertz (1857–94), a German physicist who investigated oscillations in electromagnetic radiation. The sidebar above discusses frequency and its relation to other important properties of waves.

ing equation involving frequency, f, wavelength, λ, and the speed, c, of the wave:

$$f\lambda = c.$$

By dividing both sides of the equation by f, one gets $\lambda = c/f$. For a given speed, the frequency and wavelength are inversely proportional. This means that as one of these properties increases, the other must decrease.

Frequency is related to a wave's energy—the higher the frequency, the higher the energy. (Due to the relation between wavelength and frequency, wavelength is also related to energy—the shorter the wavelength, the higher the wave's energy.) The frequency-energy relation makes sense when one considers events that generate waves, such as, for instance, a person creating a wave along a rope by swinging one of the ends. High-frequency waves require more effort and more energy, since the person must swing his or her arm faster in order to produce more cycles per second. A maker of high-frequency waves will tire sooner than a person who makes waves at a low, lazy frequency.

An important feature of waves is that particles do not travel all the way along the wave. A wave is the motion itself; in a string, for example, the individual segments bob up and down but do not move along the string very much. A wave does not transport particles or matter from one point to another, but instead a wave carries energy and momentum in the up-and-down, side-to-side, or back-and-forth vibrations along the length of its path.

All objects vibrate when they are struck, and they do so at specific frequencies. The frequency with which an object vibrates most strongly is called its *natural frequency*. People use this name because it is "natural" for the object to vibrate at this frequency, and everything has a natural frequency. For any given object, size, mass, structure, and composition determines the natural frequency in complicated ways.

People can ring bells by shaking them, causing the clapper—a small piece of metal hanging inside—to strike the side of the bell. The sound a bell makes depends on many factors, such as its size and dimensions, its composition, and its geometrical structure.

People say that when the Liberty Bell was struck, it made the musical note called E-flat.

Bells usually vibrate at frequencies that are pleasant to hear—bell makers design them that way—but just about any frequency is possible. Objects called tuning forks oscillate at a specific frequency (their natural frequency), and musicians use them to tune instruments. A tuning fork makes a pure note, which is a sound at a single frequency, and acts as a reference to which the musician adjusts an instrument in order to match the frequency. A tuned instrument makes the correct frequencies when a musician plucks a chord or taps a key.

Natural frequencies are also critical to the phenomenon called *resonance*. As mentioned earlier, an object tends to vibrate most strongly at its natural frequency when it is struck—a single blow from a hammer will set an object vibrating at several different frequencies, but the most prominent is the natural frequency. Something especially interesting happens if an object is struck repeatedly with a frequency that is the same as the object's natural frequency: the object begins to oscillate strongly, so the periodic motion has a large amplitude. Stimulating an object at its natural frequency causes it to resonate, and the oscillations have an amplitude much greater than they would have if the object was stimulated at another frequency.

Resonance is the reason that an oscillating tuning fork will cause vibrations in other, nearby tuning forks that have the same natural frequency. Because the sound of the first tuning fork stimulates the others at their natural frequency, the stimulated tuning forks resonate. Sound is not normally strong enough to cause a tuning fork to vibrate, and it will not cause tuning forks with a different natural frequency to vibrate very much. The sound has to be at or close to the natural frequency.

Resonance plays a role in engineering, if only because engineers often want to avoid it. The high accelerations experienced by airplanes and rockets cause vibrations, and if these vibrations are at or near a vehicle's natural frequency, then the amplitude may become so great as to tear the structure apart. Engineers and physicists were worried that this would happen to the huge rocket Saturn V, which lifted the Apollo astronauts from Earth, because of the massive forces involved in its acceleration. They took great care to eliminate resonances when they designed the rocket. A car's suspension system also needs to be designed so that its natural frequency is not the same as the vibrations created by road bumps or other sources. If it is, the ride is not a smooth one since the vibrations will have an amplitude capable of jolting passengers out of their seats.

Marching soldiers typically march in step but will often be ordered to break stride when crossing a bridge. This can create a lot of confusion in the soldiers, who are highly trained marchers, but resonance must be avoided. The synchronized stamping of the soldiers' feet could set up resonance in the bridge, leading to a weakening of the structure and, possibly, its collapse. Resonance is also responsible for the ability of a singer to shatter glass. If a musical note is at the natural frequency of a glass, the vibrations are so strong that the glass breaks apart.

Oscillations are important in the world for a lot of reasons. Even the ground can oscillate, usually with unfortunate consequences.

Earthquakes

When Earth formed it consisted of hot gas and molten rock and metal. As it cooled, the surface hardened and cracked, forming a number of large islands or "plates" that remain today, slowly moving about in the squishy interior. These massive plates can bump up against each other or grind along one another's edges, creating stress. Sometimes sudden shifts in the plates relieve the stress, phenomena called earthquakes.

The energy released in an earthquake spreads out from the source, usually far below the surface, in waves called *seismic waves* (from *seismos*, a Greek word for earthquake). The waves are disturbances that travel through the rocks and soil; each little bit of rock or soil vibrates about its equilibrium position, jostling its neighbors, which in turn vibrate, and so on. The two main types of waves that travel through the interior of Earth are P-waves and S-waves. P-waves (primary waves) are faster, moving through solid substances at about 3.6 miles per second (6 km/s) and through water at about 1.2 miles per second (2 km/s). S-waves (secondary waves) travel through solids at about 1.8 miles per second (3 km/s) but do not travel through liquid.

When P- and S-waves reach the surface they create two types of surface waves: Rayleigh waves (named for British physicist John William Strutt, Lord Rayleigh), which have high amplitudes and low frequencies, and Love waves (named for British mathematician A.E.H. Love), which have characteristics similar to S-waves. Love waves are the ones that cause most of the shaking that people feel during an earthquake.

The source of an earthquake is called a focus or hypocenter. This spot is where the disturbance originates. Seismic waves travel in all directions from this point, but generally they first reach the surface directly over the focus, which is called the epicenter. But the waves are picked up by recording instruments called seismographs from a wide area, depending on the strength of the earthquake, and from this data scientists can locate the focus with considerable accuracy.

Scientists use several different scales to measure earthquake magnitudes. Perhaps the most common is the *Richter scale,* named after Charles Richter, who proposed the scale in 1935. The Richter magnitude depends on the amplitude of the waves, and since the scale is logarithmic, a one-point increase in magnitude corresponds to a tenfold increase in vibration. The greatest recorded magnitude (as of October 2006) is a 9.5 earthquake that struck Chile in 1960. But the amount of damage depends as much on where the earthquake hits and the preparation of the population as it does on the severity of the oscillations.

In a region where earthquakes are frequent, there must be strict regulations concerning the strength and design of buildings. In any earthquake, it is not the ground motion itself that is dangerous to people. The danger comes from objects that collapse on top of people or give way underneath them. The San Andreas Fault, along the west coast of California, is a fissure where two plates meet and is the site of a lot of earthquakes. California has experienced many earthquakes in the past, and building construction there must meet codes designed to minimize damage during future earthquakes.

The earthquake in San Francisco, California, on April 18, 1906, toppled this statue at Stanford University. The statue fell about 30 feet (9.1 m) and pierced the sidewalk like an arrow. *(U.S. Geological Survey)*

But there are problems, and architects and engineers must keep physics in mind at all phases of the design and construction, particularly of large structures. Powerful earthquakes generate a great deal of stress, swinging tall buildings like inverted pendulums. If there is a weakness at a critical spot, then the frame of the structure will break and the building will topple over. Another problem is the previously mentioned resonance, and this is one of the most difficult to treat. If a structure shakes at its natural frequency, the amplitude of the vibration rises and can become so large that almost any structure will break, no matter how strongly it is reinforced. Engineers blamed resonance for the collapse of an elevated highway during a 1989 earthquake in Oakland, California, killing dozens of people.

But earthquakes are not the only phenomena that create waves in land or water. Any impact on the surface of the planet will cause waves to spread out and register on seismographs. Even small impacts can have an effect. Planes that crash into the ground have registered on nearby seismographs at small magnitudes, such as 1.5, on the Richter scale.

Much more powerful are explosions such as volcanic eruptions. One of the strongest explosions to occur in recorded history happened at Krakatau, a small island near the coast of Sumatra in Indonesia. In August 1883, an explosion blew apart the island with such force that the roar was heard in Australia, 1,800 miles (2,880 km) to the south. Atmospheric oscillations caused by the Krakatau explosion circled around the world numerous times, and scientists in Europe and America who recorded these waves had no clear idea at first what was responsible for them. They eventually discovered that the source was an unbelievably catastrophic explosion on the other side of the world—one of the earliest instances in which scientists realized that an event initially occurring in a small region can have global effects.

Tsunamis are ocean waves caused by an underwater earthquake or a sudden shift in the sea floor. They can be just as destructive as earthquakes, as discussed in the next chapter.

Physicists study seismic waves so that architects and engineers can build safer structures, and perhaps one day people can learn to predict when an earthquake will occur. There has been little progress on such methods of prediction to date. But another reason scientists are interested in seismic waves is that these waves reveal features and aspects of Earth's interior.

All kinds of waves, whether in the air, water, or ground, behave in certain ways. For example, a boundary—a line or plane where two different regions meet—always causes some of the wave to be reflected, similar to the way that a portion of light reflects from a glass window. (Light is a wave, or at least has wavelike properties.) The difference in the boundaries may only be in density or it can be a difference in material, but whatever the boundary, some reflection occurs. The rest of the wave travels through the boundary, but the direction is slightly bent, or refracted. This is also identical to the behavior of light, which noticeably bends as it goes from air to water or vice versa.

Scientists can learn a lot about the interior of Earth by studying the behavior of seismic waves, because these waves reflect and refract depending on the nature of the ground and the boundaries between different layers. Seismic waves give scientists a means of peering inside Earth without having to pick up a shovel, and since Earth's core is too deep to reach by digging, seismology is the principal method by which to study it. Scientists have learned that this planet has a solid inner core of iron and nickel, and a molten outer core of the same metals, which is surrounded by a solid, upper mantle of silicates and a crust of rock, with a boundary (the Mohorovičić discontinuity) between the upper mantle and the crust.

The oil exploration industry also involves waves. Because the characteristics of seismic waves depend on the nature of the material in which they travel, geologists looking for oil can identify likely spots by examining seismographs. This technique would be of limited usefulness if they had to wait until an earthquake occurred in the right spot at the right time, so oil seekers make their own waves by using a detonation, a falling weight, or some sort of oscillating device.

Sound and Hearing

Some of the most useful waves are those associated with sound. Along with light, sound is one of the most important features of the world that a person's senses can detect. Objects and events make a lot of noise, by which people and animals determine the identity of an object or an event and what, if anything, should be done about it. But listeners, and their nervous systems, must consider the physics of waves in order to make accurate determinations.

When a thunderstorm is a long distance away, the thunder is a rumble, but when the thunderstorm is overhead, thunder makes a distinct crackling noise. Thunder is obviously louder when it is closer, but the sound itself is completely different—crackling when it is nearby and rumbling when it is far away. Yet thunder is the same whether it is near or far.

The answer to this puzzle can be found in the physics of sound. Anything that pushes against air will make a sound. Air is a fluid, composed of billions of molecules moving around in random motion and colliding with each other. When something pushes against these molecules, they begin to move together in the direction they were pushed. They collide and scatter against the neighboring molecules, providing a push to these molecules, which in turn collide with their neighbors. The original push gets transmitted throughout the air in the form of pressure waves as the molecules move back and forth. Ears detect these waves as sound.

An important characteristic of any pressure wave is its amplitude, which governs the loudness of the sound. Another distinguishing characteristic is how fast the molecules are moving back and forth. This is the frequency of the sound and is what people hear as pitch. High frequencies produce high pitches, such as squeals, whines, or crackling noises, whereas low frequencies produce low pitches, such as deep voices or rumbling sounds.

The pressure waves are strong near the source of the sound, so they tend to be loud. Over distance the waves spread out and weaken, so the noise becomes softer. But an interesting fact is that this weakening depends on frequency.

Most sounds are actually composed of a number of different frequencies. This is not true for pure tones, such as the ones produced by tuning forks, but most noises are a mixture of frequencies, some high and some low. These frequencies are not always heard equally, though, especially when the sound has to travel a long distance to the listener. This is because high frequencies do not tend to go as far as low frequencies since they weaken, or attenuate, more quickly, in part because their higher frequency causes more friction and loses strength or amplitude. This is why the sound of thunder is different when heard from a distance— the high-frequency components are softer and sometimes vanish entirely, with only the low frequencies remaining. Distant thunder rumbles. A person hears the high frequencies only when thunder is nearby, in which case it crackles.

Something similar happens when sound travels through material other than air. Most material will transmit sound because the pressure waves cause it to vibrate, which in turn sets the air around it in motion. Walls transmit sounds since the pressure waves on one side cause the wall to vibrate and push against air on the other side.

Acoustics

Acoustics refers to sound and hearing. In a room with excellent acoustics, all the listeners can hear speeches or music clearly. Good acoustics are not so easy to achieve, since sound waves bounce off surfaces and cause echoes that make it difficult for an audience to understand a talking person or hear the subtle notes of a concert. Sound waves can also interfere with one another; if the air pressures hit the same spot in such a way that their waves overlap and cancel each other—if the high pressure of one wave coincides with the low pressure of another—then this interference causes dead spots where nothing can be heard.

Acoustical engineers avoid dead spots by taking into consideration the frequencies of the sound waves and the distance they travel, ensuring there are few spots in the auditorium where these waves can interfere such that they cancel each other. If the engineers do a good job, there are no members of the audience who cannot hear the performance because of a "poor seat."

Echoing is another difficult problem. A sound wave bouncing off a surface can cause the original sound to be heard repeatedly. In a small enclosed room such as a shower stall, for instance, sounds bounce from one wall to another many times. At certain frequencies, the sound resonates in these small rooms, creating a louder and richer sound that makes singing voices seem much better. (Perhaps this is why a lot of people sing in the shower.) But echoing is undesirable in large auditoriums because it becomes difficult or even impossible to understand speech, and it adds unintentional noise to musical harmonies. Some auditoriums use obstacles such as hanging panels or other ornamentation to scatter sound throughout the room, thereby diffusing the echoes.

Sound can also be absorbed, particularly by materials that are full of small holes. The sound waves enter the holes, bounce around, and lose their energy. People, and especially the clothes they wear, also absorb sound, and a concert hall full of people carries sound much differently than it does when it is empty. Acoustics experts often test auditoriums and concert halls by listening to music rehearsed in front of a "dummy" audience.

But the loudness decreases, and high frequencies lose more than low frequencies. People can hear their neighbor's music through a wall, but the drums or bass tones are louder than those of a high-pitched female vocalist.

Not all sound travels through a barrier such as a wall—some of it bounces back. This causes problems for people who want to control the sound in an enclosed room, such as a symphony orchestra playing in a concert hall. The structure of these halls and their interior must be carefully designed and selected. As discussed in the sidebar on page 99, people who design music halls must know and apply a great deal of physics.

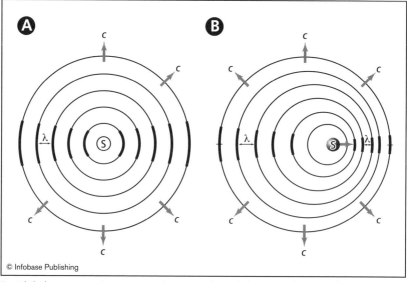

© Infobase Publishing

Part (A) shows a stationary sound source, S, emitting sound waves that go out in all directions and have the same wavelength (λ). Part (B) shows a sound source moving to the right. To a stationary observer, the sound waves in front of the source are bunched up and have a shorter wavelength (λ) than the sound waves behind the source.

Another characteristic of sound that affects the frequency is known as the Doppler effect. This effect, named after Austrian physicist Christian Doppler (1803–53), is due to motion between the source of the sound and the listener. If the source of a sound is not stationary but is approaching a listener, the listener hears the sound at a higher pitch, as shown in the diagram. The reason is that after one emitted sound wave travels away from the source, the next wave is emitted, but since the source is moving in the same direction, this sound wave is closer to the last wave than it would have been if the source was not moving. The sound waves in front of the moving source bunch together and have a shorter wavelength to a stationary observer, which results in a higher frequency. This result also occurs for similar reasons when the listener approaches a stationary sound source. The opposite is true when the source recedes from the listener, or the listener recedes from the source, and the sound decreases in pitch. The Doppler effect is the reason that to a pedestrian standing on a street corner a car horn seems to rise in pitch as the car approaches him or her and then to drop in pitch as the car speeds away.

Motion is important in terms of sound for another reason. Sound has a certain speed in air, though the speed depends on pressure and temperature: at room temperature and at sea level, sound travels at roughly 760 miles per hour (1,225 km/hr). Anything trying to accelerate past this speed in air encounters a resis-

This F/A-18 Hornet pushes through the sound barrier. The photograph illustrates that the barrier aspect of the sound barrier is real, due to the buildup of pressure waves in front of the vehicle. *(U.S. Navy/Ensign John Gay)*

tance as the pressure waves build up in front of it. This is the sound barrier. A vehicle that breaks through the sound barrier and exceeds the speed of sound is said to be traveling at hypersonic speed (*hyper* meaning "beyond" and *sonic* meaning "sound").

Airplanes traveling at hypersonic speeds are convenient because they are tremendously fast, but they also produce uncomfortably loud sounds called sonic booms for people on the ground. Any plane moving through the air will make noise, but at hypersonic speed the plane leaves behind the pressure waves it creates. As the plane races ahead of its own sound it has to thrust air out of the way—the air in front of the plane is not already set in motion, because the plane is traveling faster than the speed at which pressure waves can travel. In other words, the plane is outrunning its advance guard. As a result, the air thrust aside compresses into an enormous pressure wave, called a shock wave, which is heard as a sonic boom. There is little that can be done to prevent these shock waves.

Changes in the speed of sound are also important. Sound travels much faster in water than in air, and a person can hear a whisper across a lake. Sound travels more slowly high in the atmosphere, where the air is less dense. Chuck Yeager, the first pilot to break through the sound barrier, flew at a high altitude so that he would not have to go so fast to reach hypersonic speed. The reduced density also offered less resistance to motion. Astronauts traveling in the vacuum of space need not worry about the speed of sound, because without air there can be no sound.

Sound is motion—a vibration in the air—and it has energy. This energy of vibration puts walls and other objects in small but effective motion, and it is what provides people with the sense of hearing. The pressure waves create a small vibration in a membrane, called the eardrum, in the human ear, which sets into motion an amazing device in the inner ear consisting of three tiny bones and a fluid-filled canal. This physiological system is amazing because it amplifies sound so well—people can detect a sound so faint that it moves the eardrum only the distance of about the diameter of an atom (0.1 nm).

The energy in sound has also been used with excellent results in a number of technological devices. Because at least part of a sound wave reflects from obstacles and boundaries, sound can be used to explore an environment in which vision is of little use. In the past, sailors traveling at night or in fog-bound waters would stand at the bow, call out in a loud voice, and listen for any echoes. A returning echo meant there was an obstacle ahead. Modern technology has dispensed with the need to use sound in this way, and these days people use sonar (the word stands for *so*und *na*vigation *r*anging). Sonar emits pulses of sound and uses the reflections to reveal any objects in the surrounding area. In World War II, sonar detected the presence of underwater submarines and mines. Today, sonar has advanced to such a degree that precision maps can be made of the ocean floor.

But nature has been using sonar for a lot longer, as discovered by scientists who noticed that bats could fly while blindfolded, but not with blocked ears. A bat with earplugs is unable to navigate and flies into walls or other obstacles—bats "see" where they are going not with their eyes but by listening for the echoes of ultrasonic squeaks they emit. The word *ultrasonic* means "beyond sound" and refers to sound waves with a frequency too high for humans to hear. The highest audible frequency for most people is less than 20,000 Hertz, while bats typically emit sounds at several times this frequency. Although high frequencies cannot be used over long distances because of attenuation, they give the bat a better "picture" because they carry more information. Other animals, including porpoises, also employ this method, particularly while hunting small fish in murky water.

Harmonics: The Sound of Music

Bats and porpoises "see" with sound, but humans put sound to yet another purpose, which may not be as practical but which gives many people a great deal of pleasure. This purpose, music, relies on physics as much as sonar does, though the judge of a pleasurable listening experience is in the ear and brain of the listener.

The pressure changes that comprise a sound wave can be picked up by a microphone and transformed into an electrical signal. The signal reproduces the sound's pressure waves as variations in electric current or voltage. When a pure tone such as the output of a

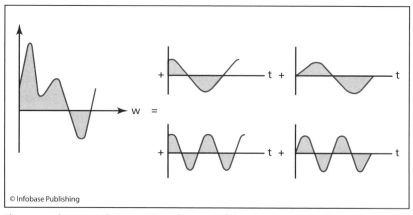

© Infobase Publishing

The wave shown at the top, *W,* is the sum of the sine waves shown at the bottom. This means that at each time (*t*), adding together the amplitudes of all the sine waves gives the amplitude of *W.* The sine wave amplitudes can be positive, negative, or zero; a sum of values of the same sign results in a higher amplitude for *W,* but adding positive and negative values of equal magnitude results in a zero amplitude for *W.*

tuning fork is recorded, the signal looks like a *sine wave,* a special type of wave. Several centuries ago a French mathematician, Jean-Baptiste-Joseph Fourier (1768–1830), discovered that all waves, no matter how complicated, are the sum of a lot of sine waves of varying frequency and amplitude, as shown in the figure above. Fourier developed a formula to find the sine waves for any given waveform. Today this method is called Fourier analysis.

As applied to sound waves, what this means is that any sound is composed of a sum of pure tones (sine waves) or, in other words, a sum of different frequencies. A particular sound may require a huge number of sine waves or it may require only a few; if the sound requires only one frequency then it is a pure tone, a sine wave. Describing a sound in terms of its sine wave content is called frequency analysis, because the process breaks sound down into its component frequencies (sine waves).

Frequencies are important characteristics of sound, as mentioned earlier, and they are especially vital in music. Musical instruments make sound, but they generally do not make sound of a single frequency. The pressure waves of instruments are more complicated than just a single sine wave; they are richer, containing multiple frequencies. But in many cases the frequencies made by musical instruments are related to one another, and this relationship is critical in understanding the physics of music.

A violin is a good example. A violin consists of strings tied down at both ends. When a string begins vibrating, as it does when a bow crosses it, the string cannot move at either end, so all the movement is done by other parts of the string. Fourier said that no matter what sort of movement the string makes, it can be thought of as a sum of sine waves. But in the case of the string that is tied down at both ends, the sine waves cannot be of any frequency—the wave must fit on the string, since neither end can move. There is a lowest possible frequency, which occurs in the simplest possible motion—the middle of the string vibrates up and down. All other possible frequencies that the string can make are integer multiples of this frequency, which is called the fundamental frequency. The other frequencies are equal to the fundamental multiplied by some whole positive number, such as 3. These are called *harmonics.*

The harmonics of a musical instrument provide its unique sound. A listener can tell the difference between a piano and a violin even when they play the same note, because each instrument has a unique set of harmonics. The blend of these harmonics creates a rich texture, with certain mixtures having a pleasant sound to most listeners. Some instruments make music but lack this harmonic structure: drums and cymbals vibrate at a mixture of frequencies but not in the same way that a stringed instrument such as a violin does. Music has many forms.

Another important aspect of a stringed instrument is that it is not the actual strings that produce most of the sound. A vibrating string pushes air and makes a sound, but not a loud one since the string is thin and cannot push much air. The music from a stringed instrument comes mostly from the sounding board, set into motion by the movement of the string. (Electronic instruments, however, use electrical signals to drive the speakers.) The quality of the sounding board is therefore critical to the quality of the music. An instrument maker named Antonio Stradivari, who lived in the 17th and 18th centuries, made violins and other string instruments that sounded so wonderful that many musicians consider them to be of the highest quality ever created.

Harmony in music comes from the multiple pitches, which sound pleasing to the human ear when heard together. Not all sounds are pleasant to all ears, and exactly what sort of sound is musical and what is not depends on one's culture and preference. Traditional music in Europe and America uses specific ratios of pitches—a musical scale—that to many people in these cultures are the most harmonious.

Synthesizers: Machines That Talk

Speech, like music, is found in all cultures. HAL, the computer in the 1968 movie *2001: A Space Odyssey*, could talk as well as a person. But obviously HAL had no vocal cords, nor did "he" possess any of the other physiological equipment that people use to talk. In humans, speech is the result of air forced through the vibrating folds in the top of the trachea (windpipe), and out between the lips, which along with the rest of the mouth and the tongue are shaped to produce specific sounds. HAL contained a *synthesizer,* a machine that artificially produces speech.

Today's speech synthesizers do not sound quite as good as the fictional HAL. The earliest synthesizers mimicked human biology, with mouth cavities and vibrating chords. This approach to creating speech is similar to the early attempts to achieve flight by mimicking birds. But then scientists and engineers realized there are better ways to generate artificial speech. One common method is to stitch the components of speech together: synthesizers use prerecorded syllables and play them one after another to make words, or sometimes they put words together to make sentences. The other way is to make speech from scratch by mixing together frequencies electrically and sending the signals to a loudspeaker to transform the signals into sounds.

There are several difficulties in synthesizing speech that currently prevent engineers from building a talking computer as effective as HAL. Frequency analysis shows that human speech is complicated. Although most people's voices contain a few dominant frequencies—low for men (who generally have deep voices) and high for women—there are a number of different frequencies involved for each speech sound. Matching the rhythm and variation of human speech is difficult. People do not speak with flat voices; some words are accented, the pitch may be different, the rate may vary, and all these factors depend on context. A question sounds different than a statement, and an angry person sounds different than a tired one.

Another difficulty is with language itself. Although the speech synthesizer can generate the sound of a word, sometimes the same word has a different sound (and meaning). For instance, a hunter uses a bow and arrow, but performers bow to an audience. Even fast and sophisticated computers have a lot of trouble figuring language out, because so much depends on context.

Music, on the other hand, is much simpler to synthesize. Electronic music synthesizers are able to imitate most musical instruments quite well by mixing together frequencies and sending the combined signal to a loudspeaker. This is commonly done in computers to make various sounds to alert the user or to provide multimedia events, and especially for the sounds and music of computer games. There is even a specific type of computer file created to store synthesized music, called the Musical Instrument Digital Interface (MIDI) file. MIDI files do not contain the actual music but rather the instructions by which a synthesizer can produce it. This makes MIDI files much smaller in size than a file containing an actual audio recording, and they take up much less storage space on computer disks.

Ultrasound Imaging: Seeing with Sound

Seeing with sound is not just for the navy and mammals such as bats and porpoises. Physicians see with sound as well.

Ultrasound imaging is an excellent way to see inside the human body without performing surgery. It is a noninvasive procedure, meaning that no probes or instruments are inserted into the body. Noninvasive procedures are preferable to invasive ones because there is generally little pain and discomfort, and no risk of infection.

But to get a quality picture, this technique must use high-frequency sound waves, the fast vibrations of which reveal a lot of information and detail of the object to be imaged. The operator brings a sound generator, which works similar to a loudspeaker, into contact with the patient. The sound penetrates harmlessly and painlessly into the body, where some of the energy reflects from tissue boundaries and organs. A device that has a function similar to a microphone picks up this reflected energy and converts it into electrical signals. The properties of the reflected waves provide information on the shape and condition of the tissues from which the waves bounced. As with sonar, ultrasound uses sound echoes to form an image of objects that are otherwise invisible to the human eye.

The term *ultra* suggests that ultrasound imaging uses sound waves that are beyond the hearing range of most humans, and this happens to be true. The frequency in many cases is in the millions of Hertz, well beyond the normal hearing range. Ultrasound is effective for examining internal organs and is often used for the heart, abdominal organs, eyes, and blood vessels. It is also frequently used to find possible sources of pain or swelling in the body. But one of the most common applications of ultrasound is to image the fetus in the womb of a pregnant woman, and ultrasound is a tremendous help to a physician in determining the health and development of the fetus. Another advantage of ultrasound is that because the images can be produced quickly, they can be made into a movie, allowing the user to view and study movements.

Since many materials, including air, attenuate high frequencies, ultrasound has limitations, especially since it uses extremely high frequencies. Bones are not good conductors of ultrasound because they strongly attenuate high frequencies. Ultrasound would be a splendid tool to image the brain, but it is not possible to obtain detailed images of the brain because the skull prevents most of the sound's energy from reaching the target. Ultrasound also cannot penetrate air, which is the reason why the operator applies a gel to the patient's skin before the procedure. The gel occludes air, so there is nothing between the probe and skin to keep the sound from penetrating the body.

Sound is important for both hearing and, with the help of equipment like sonar and ultrasound, for seeing as well. Scientists have also used vibrations of the ground—earthquakes—to peer into the interior of the Earth. Vibrations reveal something about the nature of all objects, because everything has a natural frequency and will resonate if it is stimulated at this rate. The world is full of oscillation, and by studying important properties such as frequency, physicists and physicians have a much better insight into how things work.

7

FLUIDS AND OBJECTS THAT MOVE IN THEM

THE OCEAN STRUCK with an awesome force on December 26, 2004, when an Indian Ocean tsunami slammed into coastlines across much of southern Asia and parts of Africa. About 250,000 people perished and millions were left homeless. On August 29, 2005, Hurricane Katrina devastated the city of New Orleans, flooding 80 percent of the city, killing hundreds of people and leaving thousands more stranded in rising water. Tragedies such as these strongly motivate the study of the physics of fluids.

Physicists use the term *fluid* for both air and water because they have similar properties. The forces exerted by air and water are extremely important not only in tsunamis and hurricanes but also in daily life. Airplanes and ships experience forces as they move through air or water, and these forces must be understood for efficiency and safety reasons. But sometimes the forces acting on objects traveling in fluids cause strange things to happen, such as the flight of a baseball pitcher's curveball. This chapter explores the powerful and sometimes odd behavior of fluids, and the objects that move in them.

To study fluids, physicists of the past have performed many notable experiments. Some of these experiments involve a measurement that is especially important in determining the proper-

Hurricane Katrina put about 80 percent of New Orleans, Louisiana, underwater in August 2005. *(U.S. Army/Coast Guard/Petty Officer 2nd Class Kyle Niemi)*

ties of a fluid—the measurement of pressure, or how much force it exerts on an area. The results of these experiments were often surprising.

Air and Water Pressure

In the 17th century, Otto von Guericke, a German scientist and politician, made a hollow sphere by putting together two small hemispherical pieces of metal. The hollow sphere was like a small globe and the two halves—the hemispheres—easily pulled apart. But after von Guericke pumped out most of the air inside the sphere, the hemispheres stuck together as if glued. It was almost impossible to pull the pieces of metal apart, and even the huge force generated by two teams of horses, which could easily haul a coach full of people, could not separate the hemispheres. But the two halves simply fell apart when air was let back inside the sphere.

What von Guericke found was the strength of the atmosphere's pressure. The air surrounding the planet was acting on the two halves of the sphere, holding them together, and this force came from the air molecules. Fluids such as air are composed of a gigantic number of molecules, all in motion and bouncing off each other and other objects. When von Guericke removed most of the air inside the sphere, few molecules remained to push against the interior, but the atmosphere continued to act on the outside. A huge number of molecules hit the outer surface of the sphere, pushing the halves together, while few were hitting the inside. A single molecule contributes an extremely small force by itself, but large numbers of them add up, and this was the force the horses were fighting against when they tried to pull the sphere apart.

Force, F, pressure, P, and the area, A, on which the force acts are related by the equation $P = F/A$. The equation says that pressure is inversely related to the area on which a given force acts—the smaller the area, the greater the pressure. The equation for pressure is general and holds for any material, not just fluids. People use snowshoes, which increase the area of contact with the snow, to decrease the pressure so their feet will not sink too deeply into snow. This is also the reason experienced outdoorsmen crawl instead of walk when forced to travel on dangerously thin ice.

Atmospheric pressure is important in a lot of ways that, as in von Guericke's sphere experiment, seem unusual. Sipping a beverage with a straw involves atmospheric pressure, although many people do not realize it. The jaw and tongue muscles create a partial vacuum in the mouth, and the atmosphere pushes the liquid up the straw. The molecules of the atmosphere are constantly pushing against the liquid and drive it up the straw because there are few molecules of air in the mouth to stop it, just as the atmosphere clamped von Guericke's sphere when he pumped out the air. This only works when the beverage is in an open container, or at least partly exposed to air; trying to use a straw to sip liquid from a sealed container would be ineffective.

The same process was responsible for the development of the barometer, an instrument used to measure air pressure. When early scientists filled a long thin tube with a liquid and inverted it while placing the open end underneath the surface of a liquid in a tub, some, though not all, of the liquid ran out of the tube and into the tub. Atmospheric pressure supported the weight of the liquid remaining in the tube, acting on the surface of the liquid in the tub.

But atmospheric pressure can only support a certain amount of weight. In the 17th century, Italian physicist Evangelista Torricelli (1608–47) made a barometer using mercury, and he showed that the atmospheric pressure can support a column of mercury 30 inches (760 mm) high. Torricelli used mercury instead of water because it is 13.6 times heavier than water. The height of water that the atmosphere can support is therefore 13.6 times 30 inches or almost 34 feet (10.4 m); if he had used water, Torricelli would have had to make a much longer tube than he wanted. This also means that no one can use a straw longer than 34 feet (10.4 m) vertically to sip water, because the atmosphere cannot push water that high. This is not a limitation that will trouble many people, although it does explain why the vacuum pumps of early miners failed to raise water more than about 34 feet (10.4 m), much to their dismay.

As physicists refined the barometer and made it more precise, they discovered that atmospheric pressure is variable. Air pressure fluctuates, and although the fluctuations are small, usually less than 1 percent, they are important because they can be used to predict the weather. Storms arise in or around these fluctuations, and so weather forecasters often talk about areas of high pressure and low pressure.

Balloonists discovered one of the most important things about atmospheric pressure when they became dizzy and fainted if they ascended too high. The reason, they quickly realized, was a lack of oxygen. At high altitudes there is too little pressure and not enough air to breathe.

The air gets thinner at increasing heights because the atmosphere is composed of molecules flying every which way, and molecules tend to travel from places that have more molecules to places that have fewer—they move down their *concentration gradient*. Air tends to move up and away from the surface and out into space, and although gravity works against this tendency, gravity's strength decreases with distance so that it holds on to more air closer to the surface of the planet. The atmospheric pressure at a height of about 5,570 feet (1,700 m), which is roughly the altitude of Denver, Colorado, is only about 80 percent that of sea level. On the top of Mount Everest, with an altitude of 33,630 feet (8,850 m), the atmospheric pressure is less than 30 percent of sea level. Airplanes often fly at heights in which the atmospheric pressure is 30 percent or less of sea level, and people who go this high must take some air with them to compensate for the low pressure. Jetliner cabins are pressurized so the passengers can get enough oxygen to breathe, and mountain climbers have to carry oxygen tanks along with them.

Some physicists like to think of the atmosphere as an ocean of air. The pressure it exerts on any point is due to the weight of the air above that point, pressing down on the things below. When standing or walking on the surface of the Earth, everyone supports a tall, thin column of air that, fortunately, is not dense and weighs little.

The ocean analogy is a good one, because the pressure that water exerts on objects beneath the ocean works in a similar way to that of atmospheric pressure. Water, being much heavier than air, exerts a greater pressure. (Another difference is that unlike the atmosphere, which thins out at high altitudes, water has a more uniform density from the top of the sea to the bottom.)

The equation above can be used to calculate water pressure. The force, F, that water exerts because of its weight is equal to its mass, m, times the acceleration due to gravity, g. Since the mass of water equals its density, d, times the volume (which is area, A, times height, h), $P = F/A = mg/A = dAhg/A = dhg$. The pressure a person feels beneath the surface of water depends only on two constants—d, the density of water, and g, the acceleration due to gravity—and the height of water above. As long as the water density remains roughly the same, the pressure depends only on depth. Shape is unimportant, so water pressure acts on every point of a submerged object with the same strength, provided the points are at about the same depth.

In actual numbers, $d = 1$ gram per cubic centimeter, and $g = 32$ feet/second^2 (9.8 m/s^2), but water pressure is easiest to think about when compared to atmospheric pressure. For each 33 feet (10 m) a diver descends into the water, the pressure increases by the equivalent of one atmosphere (the pressure of the atmosphere at sea level). At 330 feet (100 m), the pressure from the water is 10 times stronger than atmospheric pressure at sea level. Considering the trouble von Guericke's horses had with only one atmosphere, this is an amazingly strong pressure. At that depth even teams of whales would have a hard time separating two halves of an empty sphere.

The powerful water pressure explains the difficulty of underwater travel. Even modern submarines cannot safely descend much below 2,300 feet (700 m); the record for the deepest ocean dive

Trieste II, launched in 1965, was designed to dive to depths of 20,000 feet (6,100 m). *(NOAA/OAR/NURP)*

is an astounding 35,800 feet (10,915 m), achieved in 1960 by Auguste Piccard and Donald Walsh in a specially designed submersible. The strength of water pressure also explains why cities build storage tanks high off the ground, because the water in these water towers is high enough so that its pressure helps drive the fluid through pipes and into homes. And water pressure explains the problems encountered by engineers who design water systems in skyscrapers. Without careful placement of pumps and controls, the top-floor occupants would only get a trickle from the faucet, and people on the bottom floor would get a flood.

Water pressure affects humans in many other ways. Underwater divers cannot swim to the surface too quickly, due to the huge difference between the pressure at the surface and the pressure deep under the water. The reason is because of a gas called nitrogen that is dissolved in the blood. The amount of dissolved gas depends on pressure—higher pressure means more dissolved gas. If a person goes too quickly from a high pressure environment to a low one, some of the nitrogen dissolved in the blood will rapidly leave the

This water storage tank in Pennsylvania towers over the surrounding trees. The pressure helps keep water flowing through the pipes. *(Kyle Kirkland)*

solution and form bubbles in the bloodstream that can block circulation. This dangerous process is called decompression sickness (also known as the bends).

An understanding of fluid pressure is also important in physiology, because the vascular system—the blood vessels—forms an enclosed system filled with fluid (blood) that has a pressure acting on the blood vessel walls. This pressure is called blood pressure, and its value depends on several factors such as the diameter of the vessels, the amount of blood, and the activity of the heart. The heart is a powerful muscle whose job is to circulate the blood, and one of the things it has to fight against is gravity. Considering the weight of blood, there can be quite a difference between the blood pressure in a person's head and feet when standing upright. (And when upside down, people often say that the blood is "rushing" to their head.) Physicians usually measure blood pressure at the upper arm, which is about the same height as the heart.

Ocean Waves, Tsunamis, and Tides

Blood pressure is vital but not great in magnitude—there is not a huge amount of blood in the human body—but fluid can unleash tremendous forces. The destructive force of water was clearly evident in the Indian Ocean tsunami of December 26, 2004.

The word *tsunami* is from the Japanese words for harbor (*tsu*) and wave (*nami*). A tsunami is actually a series of waves that travel at speeds of up to about 600 miles per hour (960 km/hr) in deep water and attain heights of up to 100 feet (30.5 m) or more when they strike land. The 2004 tsunami had a speed of about 500 miles per hour (800 km/hr) while traveling through deep ocean waters, and as the tsunami came ashore it reached heights of 30 feet (9.1 m) and even 90 feet (27.4 m) in some places.

As in all water waves, it is the energy that travels in a tsunami, not the water. The water does move, of course, but mostly in a vertical motion, up and down, with only a small horizontal movement.

Tsunamis get started by dramatic events, a much different process than for typical, surface waves. Ocean waves can have many sources, but the most common source is wind. As the wind blows across the surface of the water, friction acts between the moving air molecules and the water below. The water begins to move in a circular motion, up and down and also with a little sideways movement. It jostles its neighbors, which are also set into motion, and the wave moves from region to region along the surface of the water.

In contrast, a sudden and powerful disturbance in the ocean, such as an undersea earthquake, generates tsunamis. Ocean waves driven by wind are mostly limited to the surface, but tsunamis extend well into the depths. The 2004 tsunami developed because of a strong earthquake whose center was in the sea, near the coast of the Indonesian island of Sumatra. The earthquake measured 9.0 on the Richter scale, one of the largest ever recorded.

The sudden movement of the earth under the water creates the immensely strong tsunami, a process similar to that of the ripples produced by a stone thrown into a pond. With the ripples, the stone pushes into the surface to create the waves; in the case of a tsunami, the earthquake suddenly pushes the water upwards, as if a stone were being thrown from the depths, toward the surface. The water, being incompressible, forms a wave that radiates away from the initial disturbance, like the ripples on a pond. But the tsunami is much stronger.

Tsunamis travel quickly because the force that generates them is powerful, and because they move through the whole depth of the ocean. Such huge volumes of water exert strong forces, requiring little time to exert their effects. In the deep sea, a tsunami does not rise very high; the wave may be unnoticeable to the crew of a vessel in the middle of the ocean, as it is perhaps a swell of only two or three feet (less than one meter). Although the energy of the wave is tremendous, it involves such a large mass of water that there is not much movement. But then the wave gets to shallow water, and when it does a tsunami attains a great height. The tsunami wave in deep water consists of a small movement of a massive column of water, but as the wave travels into shallow water near the coast, the mass of the column is much smaller. The energy of the wave, which was set into motion by the disturbance, can move a giant column of water by a little, or a small column of water by a lot.

The tide is out in this photograph of the coastline at the Bay of Fundy. *(Elizabeth Kirkland)*

Not all seismic activity under the ocean produces a tsunami. Scientists need a better understanding of the physics of fluids so that they can predict what sort of activity will cause a tsunami, and how destructive it will likely be. Accurate forecasts are essential if disasters such as the tsunami of 2004 are to be avoided in the future.

Tides also affect shorelines, although much more gently. Unlike wind waves and earthquake-driven tsunamis, the gravitational pull of the Moon (and to a far lesser extent, the Sun) produces the tides. This force causes bulges to form in the ocean, which move as Earth rotates. Tides have a small effect in the middle of the ocean, where the difference between high tide and low tide is only about three feet (less than 1 m), but can have a large effect on a coast. The shape of the shore and ocean floor has a tremendous influence on how much the water will rise; high tide in the Bay of Fundy in Canada can rise 50 feet (15.2 m) above the low-tide level.

How Hurricanes Move

Hurricanes are as destructive as tsunamis, but the physics of these ocean storms are quite a bit different. Hurricanes form in warm tropical waters with a temperature of at least 80°F (27°C). Winds swirl around a central eye, which is an area of extremely low atmospheric pressure; a storm in which these winds consistently blow with a speed of 74 miles per hour (119 km/hr) or more is called a hurricane. (If the wind speed is less, the storm is called a tropical storm or a tropical depression.) Scientists classify hurricanes in categories based on the maximum sustained winds, and a category 5, the most powerful, has continuous winds of at least 155 miles per hour (249 km/hr). Most of the hurricanes in the Atlantic Ocean begin as thunderstorms on the west coast of Africa and strengthen as they move over the warm tropical waters.

Forecasting the path of these powerful storms is important. A hurricane in 1900 devastated the city of Galveston, Texas, and the residents had no warning. Strong winds and waves lashed the shoreline, flooding the streets and houses. A staggering number of people, estimated at 6,000–8,000, lost their lives in one of the deadliest natural disasters in American history.

Storm prediction and warnings have greatly improved since 1900. Much has been learned from the observations of satellites and measurements taken aboard hurricane-hunting airplanes. Hurricanes do not simply follow a random direction, but are "steered" by pressures and winds high in the atmosphere. As noted in the first section of this chapter, air pressure in the atmosphere varies slightly at different times and in different places. When Hurricane Ivan swept across the Caribbean in 2004, forecasters accurately predicted its path because of a large mass of air at high pressure located near the Bahamas. This air pushed and guided Ivan to take the path that it did in this region.

But the job of meteorologists is not always that easy, and the movement of hurricanes is seldom consistent. For example, when Ivan moved into the Gulf of Mexico, there were suddenly no clear forces to guide it, so its trajectory became much more uncertain. Variable winds and pressures in high altitudes create situations in which weather forecasters cannot be sure exactly where the storm is going, and as a result, the predicted path is a broad area. Forecasts three days in advance typically show paths that are several hundred miles wide, with no indication precisely where in this area the hurricane will actually hit. In 2005 upper-level winds pushed Hurricane Katrina north through the Gulf of Mexico and onto the Mississippi and Louisiana coast, where forecasters correctly predicted landfall to within 20 miles (32 km) almost two days in advance—an unusual accuracy—but they did not foresee a last-minute turn in the track.

Due to the improvements of storm-prediction methods and technology since 1900, preparation and evacuations have decreased the damage and reduced the loss of life from hurricanes. But the uncertainty in the long-range forecasts means that a large region must respond to the emergency, even though not all the people will ultimately be affected. The larger the population that must prepare, the costlier and more disruptive these preparations will be. Florida was struck by four hurricanes in 2004, and nearly all of the state's coastal population was involved in at least one of them. Katrina flooded New Orleans, Louisiana, in August 2005, devastating the city. Although the uncertainty over where a hurricane will hit the shore decreases as it gets closer, there is a need for consistently accurate forecasts farther in advance of the storm's arrival, though chaos, as described in chapter 2, places a limit on predictions. The physics of atmospheric pressure, winds, and circulation patterns is complicated, and more study of how fluids behave is essential to understand how hurricanes move.

Ships

Other objects that move in or over water, such as ships, are much more predictable than storms. Ships are made of wood, polymer material (plastic), and, for large vessels, steel, and their motion is easier to understand than that of a swirling wind. But the question of how wood or steel floats is an interesting exercise in physics.

Steel is a composite of iron and carbon and has a density of about 7.8 times that of water. Because of its greater density, steel should sink, which it does. But as a piece of steel sinks, there is a force exerted on it by the water. The steel sinks into the water because of gravity, but the water level rises by an amount equal to the volume displaced by the steel. The strength of the force is equal to the weight of the water that has been displaced. This force is called *buoyancy*, as described in the sidebar.

The composition of the sinking material is not relevant, since the buoyancy depends only on the volume of water displaced. If

Buoyancy

A king once asked Archimedes, perhaps the most famous scientist of the ancient world, to make sure a crown was actually made of gold, but Archimedes was not allowed to disfigure or destroy the complex shape of the crown in the process. Archimedes knew that different metals have a different density (mass/volume), but the complex shape of the crown made it impossible to measure its volume with a yardstick. Then Archimedes realized that he could accurately determine the volume by submerging the crown in water and measuring the displacement—how much the water rose. He already knew the crown's weight. From this information he could determine the crown's density and thereby its composition.

The principle that the force of *buoyancy* is equal to the weight of the displaced fluid is named in honor of Archimedes—the principle of Archimedes. Using the principle of Archimedes, a person can measure the volume of his or her finger by placing a cup of water on a weight scale and then submerging the finger in the water. The reading on the scale will increase by an amount equal to the buoyancy force, which is equal to the weight of the volume of water displaced by the finger. Knowing the density of water, a person can calculate the volume of the water, and thus the volume of the finger. The principle of Archimedes can also be used for more important measurements, such as determining the percentage of fat that a person's body contains, which is a general measure of health and athletic conditioning.

Buoyancy depends on the nature of the fluid. Denser fluid will support more weight, allowing heavier objects to float. Even water can be quite dense if there is a lot of dissolved material in it. The Dead Sea, located on the border between Israel and Jordan, gets its name because the water is so salty that few organisms can live there. The water is so dense that a person could not sink to the bottom even if he or she wanted to!

a solid steel box two feet (60.9 cm) on each side sinks in the sea, it will displace $2^3 = 8$ cubic feet (226 L) of water. This amount of water weighs almost 500 pounds (2,225 N) at Earth's surface. Since a solid steel box weighs more than this, the box will sink to the bottom of the ocean—the buoyancy force is unable to support the box's weight. But if the box is hollow, then its weight may be less than the buoyancy force. If this is the case, the box will not completely sink but will instead only displace the amount of water equal to its weight; the box will stop displacing water when the buoyancy force equals its weight. This is why a steel ship or any other type of ship can float.

People often describe ships in terms of their displacement weight. The largest ship in the world (as of March 2006) is the Norwegian tanker *Jahre Viking*, weighing more than 500,000 tons (4,450,000,000 N). The largest cruise ship at this time is the Royal Caribbean's *Freedom of the Seas* at 160,000 tons (1,424,000,000 N). The RMS *Titanic*, the marvel of its day in the early 20th century, weighed in at a mere 45,000 tons (400,500,000 N).

The physics of ships requires careful consideration during the design of such large craft. Since big ships displace a lot of water, their hulls sink deep into the ocean, and large ships must have deep harbors in order to dock. The amount of weight carried by cargo ships must also be considered, because this affects the water line (the line on the ship's hull to which the water rises). This is important because the ship must be stable, staying upright in

Workers have almost finished unloading the cargo of this ship, and the vessel's hull rests high in the water. *(Kyle Kirkland)*

strong winds and waves. Freighter ships are stable when they are carrying a lot of cargo and much of their hull is underwater, but when empty they ride high and can roll dangerously from side to side. When these ships must sail without cargo, the captain adds ballast—extra weight—to make sure that the water line is at the proper height.

Another consequence of physics is that there is a relationship between a ship's maximum speed and its stability. Ships with wide hulls are stable because they have a wide base on which to sail, so high winds and storms will not cause these ships to roll. But the wide hull means that a lot of water must be pushed aside as the boat moves forward. An efficient shape for movement through water is that of a fish (naturally enough, since such motion is vital to these creatures). Ships with thin hulls can slice through the water and achieve higher speeds, but there is a tradeoff, since these vessels are relatively unstable. Centuries ago, the Vikings built ships called longships that were fast and efficient, but the sailors had to rely on their superior seamanship to keep the vessels from capsizing in bad weather.

Physics affects how fast a propeller can turn, which along with the hull width is a factor that governs the speed of modern ships. The rotation of one or more underwater propellers powers many of today's ships, but there is a limit to how fast a propeller can turn and remain effective. When propellers turn too fast in water they tend to form air bubbles by a process called *cavitation*. The air bubbles rob the propellers of some of their energy to thrust the ship forward.

Baseballs and Golf Balls

Although the movement of ships is not too difficult to understand, the motion of other objects in a fluid can be strange enough to violate common sense. This is particularly true when the object is a spinning ball—and the outcome of a game depends on its behavior. But although common sense may be violated, the laws of physics are not.

Rotating bullets and footballs are stable in flight because of the conservation of angular momentum, as described in chapter

3. But a spinning baseball, which is round and lightweight, with stitches running along the surface, does not always fly straight. When a baseball pitcher throws a curveball, it actually does curve. Some people used to believe that this was just an illusion, but in the 1940s scientists began to film curveballs in motion to prove that it was no illusion.

A curveball gets its curve from the spin imparted by the pitcher as he or she releases the ball. The ball rotates about 18 times as it travels the standard 60 feet six inches (18.4 m) from the pitcher's mound to the plate, and the ball drags air along its surface as it spins, particularly at the raised stitches. This has two effects, both of which tend to deflect the ball. Because the spinning surface pulls some of the air along with it, one side of the ball experiences an area of low pressure that creates a force called the Magnus force (named for Heinrich Magnus, the German physicist who studied it). The dragging of air also causes the ball's wake—the air behind the moving ball—to shift, which gives the ball a push. Both of these forces act to deflect the ball in the direction of the spin. Pitchers spin the ball so that it will curve downward and a little bit to one side (a right-handed pitcher's curve ball usually curves down and to the left), and the ball loses even more altitude than would be expected if gravity were the only force acting on it.

The importance of spin can also be seen in the path of a baseball with little or no spin. When a pitcher throws a knuckleball, the ball has hardly any spin since the pitcher pushes the ball with the knuckles rather than using the palm and fingertips. A knuckleball has a wild, unpredictable flight and is tough for the batter to hit (and for a catcher to catch). Any deformity or unevenness in the ball's surface will cause knuckleballs to behave even more erratically (and will also affect curveballs as well), because the air flow is disrupted. This is why pitchers are not allowed to scratch or otherwise "doctor" the ball.

Golf is another sport greatly affected by spin. A golfer usually wants to hit a ball on a tee as far as possible, in order to get close to the green and the hole—exactly the opposite of a baseball pitcher's desire to see the ball drop in front of the batter before the pitch can be hit. The golfer gives the ball a backspin when he or she launches it from the tee, providing an extra lift. Giving the ball a topspin would be a disaster, since the golf ball would drop like a baseball pitcher's curve. Also unwanted is a spin to the right or the left, which would push the ball off a straight trajectory and toward the sand trap or pond.

Physics has shaped not only the way that golfers hit the ball but also the shape of the ball itself. Golf balls are dimpled—they have little pockmarks on their surface. The first dimpled golf ball made its appearance in the early 1900s, and the reason they were made is simple: they fly farther than smooth balls, all other things being equal.

It seems strange that a dimpled golf ball would fly farther than a smooth one. A smooth ball would appear to have an advantage because a smooth surface offers less resistance to air. Less air resistance means less drag, and so the ball might be expected to keep flying longer than a dimpled ball. That this is not true is the peculiar result of turbulent flow.

Balls with a smooth surface have greater drag overall because of their wake—a zone of swirling, turbulent air that develops behind them. Generating the wake requires energy, which can only come from the ball's motion, robbing the ball of some of its kinetic energy. Air slides easily past a smooth surface and the air molecules run into each other on the back side, forming a large wake. In contrast, dimpled balls drag some of the air along with the surface, and although this creates a certain amount of air resistance, there is a much smaller wake. As a result, dimpled balls lose less energy and fly farther.

Dimples are so important to the flight of golf balls that professional golfing associations regulate them. Newly developed balls configure the dimples in such a way to create self-correcting airflows on bad shots, so the ball flies true and far even when a golfer's swing is poor and the spin is initially wrong. Yet these balls are not allowed in most professional tournaments. Golfers apparently prefer tournaments to be a test of golfing skill rather than a test of the equipment manufacturer's knowledge of physics.

But fluid physics found a welcome use by Allied bombers during World War II, and a famous example was an air raid on the

Modne Dam in 1943. Torpedoes dropped from planes were the most effective weapons against dams, but the defenders built nets to prevent these explosives from reaching the target. The bomber's response was to use spherical or cylindrical bombs and release them into the water with a backspin. The bombs behaved like skipping stones, because the spin lifted them repeatedly out of the water. By this method the bombs avoided the defenders' nets and bounced their way across the water to destroy the dam.

Airplanes

If bombs or stones skipping in and out of a river seem strange, so does the ability of a large piece of aluminum, plastic, and steel to fly through the air. Yet airplanes manage to do so quite well.

Airplanes have improved considerably since the time of the first significant flight, which occurred in 1903 at Kitty Hawk, North Carolina, when American inventors Orville (1871–1948) and Wilbur Wright (1867–1912) stayed aloft for 12 seconds. But the principle of flying has not changed much since that time and relies on the physics of motion through fluids. The fluid in this case is air, and one of the most important principles was named after Daniel Bernoulli (1700–82), a Swiss mathematician and physicist. *Bernoulli's principle* says that a fluid's pressure decreases as its velocity increases.

Bernoulli's principle is important to airplanes because of their wings. As the airplane moves, its wings cut through the air, and some air flows across the top of the wing and some flows underneath, as shown in the figure on page 128. The wing's shape and angle of attack (the angle between the wing and the airstream through which it is moving) makes the air flowing across the top move faster. Faster-moving air has lower pressure (Bernoulli's principle), and the difference in pressure between the top and bottom of the wing develops a lifting force. If the airplane can gain enough speed so that this pressure difference becomes large, up it goes.

The lifting force demonstrated by wings is certainly not limited to airplanes. Fast-moving cars experience a similar effect, especially those whose profile is wing shaped. At high speeds a car may

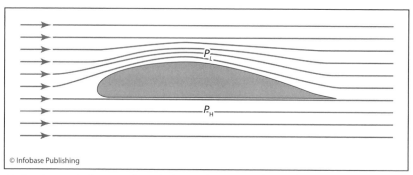

© Infobase Publishing

Air flowing past the top of an airplane wing moves faster than the air moving underneath. The air pressure on top, P_L, is lower than P_H, the air pressure on bottom, providing upward lift.

develop enough lift to cause a hazardous situation, for if the wheels are not firmly grounded then they lose traction. Race cars are vulnerable because of their tremendous speeds, so racers reduce the danger by the addition of "wings" on the car. But these wings are upside down to develop a "grounding" force instead of a lifting

The "wings" of this race car (seen in the front and the rear) are upside down compared to airplane wings, forcing the car toward the ground rather than lifting it up. This effect provides better traction and a safer race. (Panther Racing LLC)

force. Thanks to the upside-down wings, some race cars produce more than two and a half times their weight in downward force when they are at racing speed.

Bernoulli's principle has many other effects and explains why the fierce winds of hurricanes and tornadoes tend to lift the roof off houses. The air rushing past the roof has exceptionally low pressure compared to the air inside the house, so the roof experiences a lifting force, and away it goes.

Although it is tempting to attribute lifting forces solely to Bernoulli's principle, fluid motion is complicated and there is more to flying than just this one principle. There is still some debate over the details of airflow over and around wings, and more experiments and study should lead to safer, more efficient designs.

But whatever forces act to produce lift, the angle of attack is important. Too much or too little angle can lead to serious problems and the airplane stalls. Changing the angle of attack can also result in the phenomenon of an airplane flying upside down, as stunt fliers sometimes do.

Another factor in flight is the ground effect. Early in aviation history, pilots learned that lift increases when a plane flies close to Earth's surface. This is because the wing and the ground compress the air between them, increasing the pressure underneath the wing and adding to the lifting force.

Aircraft and Watercraft of the Future

By studying fluids and the forces they generate, physicists gain a better understanding of the factors that affect flying in the air and sailing in the water. This knowledge will prove valuable in the future design and engineering of aircraft and watercraft.

People have been traveling on the water a lot longer than in the air, but modern ships still have room for improvement. For instance, the cavitation problem with propellers can be avoided if a ship uses a jet for propulsion. Jets have largely replaced propellers in the air, and perhaps they will do so in the water as well. Water jets take in and then emit torrents of water, propelling the vessel by Newton's third law. Water jets are efficient and have few moving parts, so their fuel and maintenance costs are low, and they become even more efficient at high speeds, unlike propellers. Water jets typically have a rotating turbine similar to a propeller that moves the water, but higher pressures tend to keep cavitation from occurring.

Water jets have been around since the early part of the 20th century. The forward opening of the engine takes in a large quantity of water, and high-pressure pumps shoot the water out of the exhaust opening at the rear. The result is similar to the propulsion used by a squid, moving the craft forward. Water jets are often used these days in high-performance boats as well as in many small recreational vessels, but efficient pumps and high speeds are necessary for today's jets to work effectively. Few of the larger ships have as yet been fitted with this type of engine.

Large ships have other problems. Because of their mass, they sink deeper in the water. The drag this causes as the boats move in water is similar to air drag, only worse because water is heavier. Lifting the boat at least partly out of the water would avoid some of the resistance, but this requires a force. Yet lifting a boat as it moves through the water should not be any more of a problem than lifting an airplane as it moves through the air—both air and water are fluids and the process should be similar.

Lifting forces are quite common in marine locomotion, though perhaps not so well known as in flight. Sailboats are pushed by the wind, but the actual process is complicated and involves some of the same forces that generate lift on an airplane wing. A skilled crew can sail a boat upwind, an impossible feat if the only thing moving the boat is the wind pushing against the sail.

As air flows past a properly fashioned and positioned sail, the pressure in front is lower than the pressure in back. This is the same as lift, only in the case of sailboats it is not directed upward but rather forward; the sail acts like a horizontal wing, sending the vessel slicing through the water. The boat's hull can experience a similar effect. In high-stakes races such as the America's Cup, crews rely on precisely engineered sails, hulls, and rudders, as well as on their sailing skills, to carry them to victory.

Although lifting a boat out of the water is not the same thing as sailing it over the water, an underwater wing is possible and is the idea behind hydrofoils. A water foil is an underwater wing that generates a lifting force as the vessel moves, and hydrofoil boats skim the waves rather than trying to push their way through them. Perhaps one day all boats will ride the waves more efficiently.

Air travel will also continue to enjoy innovation. Jet engines for airplanes work by compressing the air coming from the intake, injecting fuel into the compressed air and igniting it, and emitting particles at high velocity to propel a craft forward. The engine needs a compressor because fuel combustion requires a lot of oxygen in a small space, so the air must be under high pressure. But when the plane is traveling at high speed, the air can compress itself as it rams into the engine, eliminating the need for a compressor. This is the basis for the ramjet engine.

The engine of a ramjet is essentially a tube. The inlet carefully funnels the air, and all that is needed is to add the fuel and ignite it. With fewer moving parts and a lighter weight, ramjets can be highly efficient machines. They require high speeds, of course—a minimum of 300 miles per hour (484 km/hr), and full efficiency needs even higher speeds. Ramjets work well at supersonic speeds (faster than Mach 1, the speed of sound) or higher, even though the engine slows the air from the intake to less than the speed of sound.

Scramjets—supersonic combustion ramjets—are ramjets whose design permits air to go through the engine at supersonic speeds. A scramjet engine can propel an aircraft to a tremendous, hair-raising velocity, but it only begins to work when the craft is already moving beyond Mach 1. The X-43, an unmanned experimental aircraft which is part of NASA's Hyper-X test program, has a scramjet engine. This experimental craft has flown several times, launched from a carrier plane (a B-52 bomber) and powered by a rocket until it is flying fast enough for the scramjet to become operable. The third test flight of the X-43A reached a record speed of 7,000 miles per hour (11,200 km/hr), or Mach 9.8, in November 2004, flying to an altitude of 110,000 feet (33,537 m). The heat from friction is so intense at this speed that the X-43A needed to cycle water behind its front edges to keep the airframe from melting.

Experimenters hope that engines like the scramjet will advance aviation technology as well as provide an easier method of reaching

A B-52 carries the X-43A toward a test of the propulsion system on November 16, 2004. *(NASA/Carla Thomas)*

low Earth orbit. As a first stage for a space vehicle—used while the craft is still traveling within the atmosphere—a scramjet engine could boost the vehicle more cheaply than does a conventional rocket. Scramjet engines have the possibility of reaching Mach 15 or higher, making the world a truly smaller place in the sense that getting from one place to another, or even into orbit, will not be as time-consuming or expensive as it has been in the past.

All the factors and mechanisms that contribute to motion through fluids are complex and sometimes difficult to understand. Fluids are complex objects themselves, and strange things occur when objects travel through air and water, or when air and water flow around objects. The downside to this is that airplanes and ships are not as efficient as they could be; the upside is that as the physics of fluids becomes better understood, aircraft and water-craft of the future will be faster, safer, and more comfortable.

CONCLUSION

THE INDIAN OCEAN tsunami of 2004 and Hurricane Katrina in 2005 are grim reminders of the impact that forces and motions can have on the world and its people. The physics of force and motion affects everyone, in big ways and small, and it will continue to do so in the future.

Many of the ideas and principles described in this book are not new, having first become known centuries ago, due to the efforts of physicists such as Galileo and Newton. But old ideas can have new applications. Sometimes the new applications are extensions of old ones, as was the case for some of the developing technology associated with the flying and sailing craft mentioned in chapters 1 and 7. Old ideas may also on occasion replace newer technology, or at least remain competitive. This could happen, for instance, if NASA decides to replace electric batteries on their newer space probes with an old-fashioned piece of rotating hardware called a flywheel.

Flywheels are wheels attached to a rotating shaft. These wheels are usually massive and heavy, and the idea of flywheels in general is to store energy in their rotation. This concept is similar to potential energy, discussed in chapter 4. Potential energy refers to energy stored in chemicals such as gasoline (chemical potential energy) or water raised to a height (gravitational potential energy), which can be extracted by various processes and which performs work.

A spinning flywheel has kinetic energy, and if the wheel is massive then it can deliver a considerable force.

Although a flywheel's kinetic energy is not the same as potential energy, one can think of the flywheel's energy as "stored," since devices can couple the wheel's motion to machines such as electric generators and transfer the energy as needed. When the machine needs energy, it draws on the flywheel's energy, which slows the flywheel's rotation; to keep the flywheel moving, energy gets transferred to the flywheel by some process. This process may occur when the machine has excess energy that it can transfer back to the flywheel, or the energy may come from another source. Flywheels were common in the past and are still found today in applications such as automobiles and generators.

NASA engineers are considering the possibility of using flywheels to store and regulate energy in future missions. Batteries are presently the most common way to store energy, but batteries tend to have disadvantages, including limited lifetimes, hazardous chemicals, and sensitivity to temperature. Researchers at NASA's Glenn Research Center in Cleveland, Ohio, and their colleagues have developed a flywheel that can spin at a rate of 60,000 rpm, the highest rotation rate yet achieved in a flywheel. This enormous rotation can store and deliver a considerable amount of energy. Engineers have yet to implement this technology but are considering using flywheels on the *International Space Station* as well as in other applications.

Other simple concepts, discussed throughout this book, also show that old ideas can have plenty of life. But there is still room for plenty of new ideas, even in an old subject like mechanics. No matter what the activity—whether at home, on the road, or on the playing field—force and motion make a difference. Studying how and why objects move is not only interesting but also profitable. An understanding of the physics of forces and motions is critical in launching astronauts, making jets fly faster, designing golf balls, choosing the string tension of a tennis racket, and pitching a curveball that drops to the dirt just as the batter takes a big, deep swing. Not everything has yet been learned, and many more forces and motions are waiting for the right observer to come along.

SI UNITS AND CONVERSIONS

Unit	Quantity	Symbol	Conversion
Base Units			
meter	length	m	1 m = 3.28 feet
kilogram	mass	kg	
second	time	s	
ampere	electric current	A	
Kelvin	thermodynamic temperature	K	1 K = 1°C = 1.8°F
candela	luminous intensity	cd	
mole	amount of substance	mol	
Supplementary Units			
radian	plane angle	rad	π rad = 180 degrees
Derived Units (combinations of base or supplementary units)			
Coulomb	electric charge	C	
cubic meter	volume	m^3	1 m^3 = 1,000 liters = 264 gallons
farad	capacitance	F	
Henry	inductance	H	

Unit	Quantity	Symbol	Conversion
Derived Units (continued)			
Hertz	frequency	Hz	1 Hz = 1 cycle per second
meter/second	speed	m/s	1 m/s = 2.24 miles/hour
Newton	force	N	4.4482 N = 1 pound
Ohm	electric resistance	Ω	
Pascal	pressure	Pa	101,325 Pa = 1 atmosphere
radian/second	angular speed	rad/s	π rad/s = 180 degrees/second
Tesla	magnetic flux density	T	
volt	electromotive force	V	
Watt	power	W	746 W = 1 horsepower

UNIT PREFIXES

Prefixes alter the value of the unit.

Example: kilometer = 10^3 meters (1,000 meters)

Prefix	Multiplier	Symbol
femto	10^{-15}	f
pico	10^{-12}	p
nano	10^{-9}	n
micro	10^{-6}	μ
milli	10^{-3}	m
centi	10^{-2}	c
deci	10^{-1}	d
deca	10	da
hecto	10^2	h
kilo	10^3	k
mega	10^6	M
giga	10^9	G
tera	10^{12}	T

GLOSSARY

acceleration a change in velocity, which can be either an increase in speed, a decrease in speed, or a change in direction

acoustics pertaining to sound

amplitude the magnitude or distance that an oscillating body has moved. The term often refers to the maximum distance or crest of a wave

angular momentum *See* MOMENTUM, ANGULAR

atmosphere the air surrounding a planet and exerting a certain pressure, which decreases with altitude; the pressure of the Earth's atmosphere at sea level is sometimes used as a standard unit of air pressure

Bernoulli's principle the principle stating that as the flow of a fluid increases, its pressure decreases

buoyancy caused by the lifting force exerted on objects placed in a fluid such as water

butterfly effect the idea that very large effects can arise from very small changes in certain systems exhibiting chaos

cavitation the formation of bubbles caused by rapid motion in a fluid

chaos the unpredictable behavior of a dynamical system that is very sensitive to changes

coefficient of restitution a measure of an object's bounciness when it collides with a hard, immobile surface, equal to the rebound speed divided by the collision speed

concentration gradient a difference in the amount or concentration of a substance across a given area or space

conservation of energy the fact that energy can be transformed into one type or another but is not destroyed

Coriolis effect a curving of an object's trajectory caused by the rotation of the Earth (or some other body on which the object is moving)

cps cycles per second

dynamical system system, composed of one or more particles, that is subject to motion or a change in conditions

elasticity the ability to return to normal size after being dented or stretched

energy the capacity to do work

energy conservation *See* CONSERVATION OF ENERGY

escape velocity the minimum velocity required to escape the gravitational pull of a planet

fluid a substance that is not solid and can flow, such as air and water

force a vector quantity that describes a push or pull, which will cause a mass to accelerate by Newton's second law unless the vector sum acting on the mass is zero

free energy machine theoretically impossible machine that would create energy out of nothing

frequency the number of cycles per unit of time for a periodic process

friction a force that resists the motion of one body against another or of one body through a medium such as air or water

geosynchronous orbit the specific orbit in which the period matches the planet's rotation

gravitation *See* UNIVERSAL LAW OF GRAVITATION

harmonics a series of frequencies in which all the values are an integer multiplied by the lowest frequency

Hertz a unit of frequency equal to one cycle per second

Hooke's law the formula describing the force exerted by many types of springs and other elastic objects: the force is proportional to the distance the spring or object is stretched or compressed

impulse a change in momentum given by a force acting over a certain period of time

inertia the property of objects with mass to resist a change in motion

initial conditions the initial state of a system, describing its position and velocity, or the value of other variables at some specified point in time. In a dynamical system these values change over time

kinetic energy the energy of an object due to its motion

mass the amount of material a body possesses, by which the body has weight when gravity acts on it and by which the body opposes or resists a change in motion

metric system a system of units based on factors of 10

moment of inertia the resistance of a body or a system to rotational motion, determined by the quantity of mass and the distance of this mass from the axis of rotation

momentum, angular a conserved vector quantity that is similar to linear momentum except that it applies to rotating bodies or systems; angular momentum is the product of the moment of inertia and rotational velocity

momentum, linear a conserved vector quantity equal to the product of mass and velocity

NASA National Aeronautics and Space Administration, a United States government agency involved in space exploration and technology

natural frequency the frequency in which a body or a system tends to oscillate when it is set in motion

Newton's first law that law that states that unless acted on by a force, a body will remain at rest or, if moving, will continue moving at a constant velocity

Newton's second law that law that states that a force causes a body to accelerate by a value equal to the force divided by the body's mass

Newton's third law that law that states that when a body exerts a force on a second body, the second body exerts an equal force on the first but in the opposite direction

orbit the path taken by an object as it revolves around another

oscillation a periodic process or movement

potential energy energy that is stored and can be transformed into kinetic energy (motion)

pressure the ratio of force to the area on which it acts

resonance the increased response of a system when acted on or driven by a process having the same frequency as the system's natural frequency

Richter scale a logarithmic scale that defines the strength of an earthquake as a single number based on the amplitude of the seismic waves

rpm revolutions per minute

satellite a body in orbit around another

scalar a quantity having a magnitude but not a direction

seismic waves oscillations caused by earthquakes

sine wave an oscillation or waveform consisting of a single frequency

SI units the system of units used by scientists. SI is an abbreviation of the French term *Système International d'Unités* (International System of Units)

stability the capacity of a system to maintain its state or return to its normal state if disturbed

superball a lively, bouncy ball, having an extremely high coefficient of restitution

synthesizer a machine that makes or constructs an object or a sequence of events such as speech or music

torque a vector quantity describing a force that will cause a body to rotate, unless the vector sum acting on the body is zero

tsunami a powerful wave created by a violent disturbance in or under the water

ultrasound sound with a frequency beyond the range of human hearing, often used for medical imaging

universal law of gravitation a law of physics describing the gravitational attraction of matter that is valid throughout the universe; the gravitational force between two bodies is proportional to the product of their masses divided by the square of the distance between their centers

vector a quantity or measurement having both a magnitude and a direction

velocity a vector indicating an object's speed and direction of travel

wavelength the distance separating maximum values (crests) of a wave

weight the result of a gravitational force acting on a object with mass

weightlessness *See* ZERO GRAVITY

work the product of force acting on an object and the distance the object moves in the direction of the force

zero gravity a term that generally refers to the apparent (but not real) absence of gravity in a freely falling object, such an object in orbit

FURTHER READING AND WEB SITES

BOOKS

Bloomfield, Louis A. *How Things Work: The Physics of Everyday Life.* 3rd ed. New York: Wiley, 2005. Easy-to-understand college-level text that covers a wide range of phenomena.

Calle, Carlos I. *Superstrings and Other Things: A Guide to Physics.* Oxford: Taylor & Francis, 2001. Explains the laws and principles of physics in a clear and accessible manner.

Davis, Susan and Sally Stephens. *The Sporting Life.* New York: Holt, 1997. Discusses the science of a variety of sports and games.

Ehrlich, Robert. *The Cosmological Milk Shake.* New Brunswick, N.J.: Rutgers University Press, 1994. A lighthearted look at the little-known physics behind some of the most curious phenomena.

Jedicke, Peter, ed. *Extreme Science: The Highway of Light and Other Man-made Wonders.* New York: St. Martin's Press, 2001. Explores topics such as advanced propulsion technology that will lead the way to the future.

Kruszelnicki, Karl. *Fidgeting Fat, Exploding Meat & Gobbling Whirly Birds.* New York: Wiley, 1999. Scientific answers to a large number of puzzling and quite often humorous questions of nature and technology.

Lee, Wayne. *To Rise from Earth.* 2nd ed. New York: Facts On File, 1999. Excellent discussion of space exploration.

Lord, John. *Sizes.* New York: HarperPerennial, 1995. Puts into perspective the vast range of sizes and magnitudes of objects.

Parker, Barry. *Isaac Newton School of Driving.* Baltimore: Johns Hopkins University Press, 2003. Splendid book describing the automobile and its devices, written with plenty of expertise and a touch of humor.

———. *Mystery of Gravity.* New York: Marshall Cavendish, 2003. Brief but excellent account of the fundamentals of gravity.

Plait, Philip C. *Bad Astronomy.* New York: Wiley, 2002. Explores a number of popular but mistaken beliefs in physics and astronomy and explains why these concepts are not scientifically valid.

Prager, Ellen J. *Furious Earth: The Science and Nature of Earthquakes, Volcanoes, and Tsunamis.* New York: McGraw-Hill, 2000. Discusses these violent phenomena, which are fascinating both in terms of their power as well as the scientific principles they exemplify.

Reithmaier, Larry. *Mach 1 and Beyond: The Illustrated Guide to High-Speed Flight.* New York: TAB Books, 1995. The physics of jets and their flight.

Reynolds, David West. *Apollo: The Epic Journey to the Moon.* New York: Harcourt, 2002. Beautifully illustrated account of the Apollo voyages to the Moon.

Smil, Vaclav. *Energies.* Cambridge, Mass.: MIT Press, 1999. A look at energy and how its many forms shape and contribute to civilization and the environment.

Suplee, Curt. *The New Everyday Science Explained.* Washington, D.C.: National Geographic Society, 2004. Concise scientific answers to some of the most basic questions about people and nature. Richly illustrated.

Swartz, Clifford. *Back-of-the-Envelope Physics.* Baltimore: Johns Hopkins University Press, 2003. A collection of simple but intriguing calculations covering a variety of phenomena from large to small, showing the usefulness of physics and elementary mathematics in understanding the world.

WEB SITES

American Institute of Physics. "Physics Success Stories." Available online. URL: http://www.aip.org/success. Accessed on March 4, 2006. Examples of how the study of physics has impacted society and technology.

American Physical Society. "Physics Central." Available online. URL: http://www.physicscentral.com. Accessed on March 4, 2006. A collection of articles, illustrations, and photographs explaining physics and its applications, and introducing some of the physicists who are advancing the frontiers of physics even farther.

Exploratorium: The Museum of Science, Art and Human Perception. Available online. URL: http://www.exploratorium.edu. Accessed on March 4, 2006. An excellent Web resource containing much information on the scientific explanations of everyday things.

HowStuffWorks, Inc., homepage. Available online. URL: http://www.howstuffworks.com. Accessed on March 4, 2006. Contains a large number of articles, generally written by knowledgeable authors, explaining the science behind everything from computers to satellites.

Imaginova Corporation. "Space.com." Available online. URL: http://www.space.com. Accessed on March 4, 2006. Although focusing on space exploration and technology, this Web site contains a wide range articles and photographs on physics and its applications.

National Aeronautics and Space Administration (NASA) homepage. Available online. URL: http://www.nasa.gov. Accessed on March 4, 2006. News and information from the U.S. agency devoted to the exploration of space and the development of aerospace technologies. This Web site contains a huge number of resources, including photographs, movies, and clear and accurate explanations of the science of space exploration.

Planetary Society homepage. Available online. URL: http://planetary.org. Accessed March 4, 2006. News and information from The Planetary Society, an organization committed to inspiring the exploration of space and other worlds.

United States Geological Survey. "Earthquake Hazards Program Web site." Available online. URL: http://earthquake.usgs.gov. Accessed on March 4, 2006. Charts earthquake activity around the world.

INDEX